2/15/13

I love you
could kiss you a lot!
taste of Little Rock!
Love & hugs...

P.S. Hope you Penny miss me
much as I do

MW01007344

Big Taste of Little Rock

The Junior League of Little Rock, Inc.

Big Taste of Little Rock

of

The Junior League of Little Rock, Inc.

Big Taste of Little Rock

The Junior League of Little Rock, Inc.

Published by the Junior League of Little Rock, Inc.
Copyright © 2009

Junior League of Little Rock, Inc.
401 South Scott Street
Little Rock, Arkansas 72201
501.375.5557

Food Photography: Copyright © by Ron Manville
Food Stylist: Mary Ann Fowlkes

Location Photography courtesy of Downtown Little Rock (page 13),
Clinton Presidential Center (page 43), Junior League of Little Rock (page 75),
Arkansas State Capitol (page 127), Little Rock Central High School (page 165),
and Arkansas Arts Center (page 201)

Library of Congress Control Number: 2008932148
ISBN: 978-0-9606724-4-8

Edited, Designed, and Produced by
Favorite Recipes® Press
an imprint of

FRP.

a wholly owned subsidiary of Southwestern/Great American, Inc.
P.O. Box 305142
Nashville, Tennessee 37230
800.358.0560

Art Director and Book Design: Steve Newman
Project Editor: Jane Hinshaw
Project Manager: Debbie Van Mol

Manufactured in the United States of America
First Printing: 2009
30,000 copies

Preface

"Bon appétit La Petit Roche!" That's possibly the way that the early French explorer Jean-Baptiste Bénard de la Harpe would have greeted you at a dinner in Little Rock when he first came up the Arkansas River in 1722. Established initially as a trading post with the Quapaw Indians, our community was born.

Now, nearly three centuries later, we in Arkansas's capital city have evolved with our own history, our own culture, our own traditions, and our own special foods and recipes. So that you, too, can enjoy those culinary pleasures, we of the Junior League of Little Rock are proud to present *Big Taste of Little Rock*.

Mirroring the diversity of our city, we have compiled various selections deliciously on-target for a variety of occasions—from an informal family meal to a more formal dinner with friends and associates. Plus, sprinkled throughout this adventure are slices of life and insights into the sites that make Little Rock one of the most livable, historic, and interesting places in America.

In six chapters, we are adding more than 250 recipes to your culinary collection. These selections have been created in the kitchens of our JLLR members, of our families and friends, and of local chefs. Each has been tested for taste, quality, and ease of preparation so that you can be assured of the best of our best.

Prepare to savor a big taste of our city with an incredible edible journey through the heart of the Natural State: Little Rock.

Table of Contents

12

A Taste from
Downtown

Appetizers & Beverages

Relish Little Rock's
Accomplishments

Soups & Salads

42

74

Junior League of
Little Rock:
Serving Others

Meats & Main Dishes

The Junior League of Little Rock: Making a Positive Difference

Since our founding in 1914, the Junior League of Little Rock has established a record of service that meets the needs, opportunities, and challenges within our community. For more than eight decades, the Junior League of Little Rock's successful approach to community impact has been to identify a community need; develop a project to meet that need; ensure the success of that project through the commitment of trained volunteers and funds; and at the appropriate time, turn the project over to the community. Many examples of our projects that now operate independently of the Junior League of Little Rock can be found throughout Little Rock and this cookbook. Support for these projects is provided in part through the publication and sales of our cookbooks, *Little Rock Cooks; Traditions, A Taste of the Good Life;* and *Apron Strings: Ties to the Southern Tradition of Cooking.* With the development of *Big Taste of Little Rock*, we hope to achieve the success of our previous publications.

Our mission statement continues to define our dedicated collective aim:

> *The Junior League of Little Rock, Incorporated, is an organization of women committed to promoting voluntarism, developing the potential of women, and improving the community through the effective action and leadership of trained volunteers. Its purpose is exclusively educational and charitable.*

With that mission as our foundation, we are inspired and motivated by the leadership exercised by our members throughout the years in making a positive difference for our community and state. The training provided by the Junior League of Little Rock has played a vital role in accelerating civic progress and prosperity. The following are just a few of the numerous examples.

The Junior League of Little Rock was instrumental in the creation of the Arkansas Arts Center. In the late 1950s, women of the Junior League of Little Rock, including Jeane Hamilton, set out to fill a void in the Little Rock community. For all the culture the city possessed, there was a need for an epicenter for the arts. These Junior League of Little Rock volunteers traveled throughout the state, presenting an action plan and requesting that funds be pledged. A key element in the program's success was the volunteer recruitment and leadership provided by future Governor and Mrs. Winthrop Rockefeller. As a result, in the early 1960s, the Arkansas Arts Center was founded and a headquarters was built in MacArthur Park. The arts center's reach is wide and serves not only Little Rock, but the state as a whole. The arts center continues to flourish, and so does the influence of Junior League members.

The development of Riverfest was another time when the Junior League of Little Rock stepped forward to improve our community. In the 1970s, there was a need to establish an entertainment festival. The phenomenal results speak for themselves, with Riverfest continuing to be Arkansas' largest single weekend event.

Much of this achievement can be traced to Jane Rogers, Junior League of Little Rock Riverfest Committee member and past Riverfest chairperson. Jane has utilized those same skills honed by her Junior League voluntarism in her own professional career. Disciplines like organization, the ability to create business plans, public speaking, and fund-raising—all initially nurtured by her Junior League of Little Rock experiences—have allowed Jane to achieve extraordinary success in the development efforts of a leading national women's fraternity.

And Jane's example is not singular in taking skills learned from service in the Junior League of Little Rock and incorporating them into first-class business leadership. Take a look at the career of Judy Adams in owning and operating one of Little Rock's most successful catering services and of Janet Jones in founding and managing her highly respected real estate company. Yes, their advancements were of their own making. However, they certainly point with pride to the beneficial skills that they gained early through their Junior League training.

It is these women—the Jeanes, Janes, Judys, Janets, and countless others in our membership—who define who we are and what we can accomplish together in the days ahead. With funds raised by this cookbook, programs like Stuff the Bus, GROW, Nightingales, Partners for Hope, KOTA Camp, and FACT will continue to excel.

We salute and thank each of our Junior League of Little Rock members—past, present, and future. To you, we proudly dedicate *Big Taste of Little Rock.*

—The Cookbook Development Committee of the Junior League of Little Rock

Cookbook Development Committee

Ginger Blackmon, *Chair*

Leigh Ann Crain, *Co-Chair*

Jennifer Robinson, *Marketing Chair*

Stephanie Bynum, *Recipe Coordinator*

Jenny Faulkner, *Text Coordinator*

Sydney Blackmon, *Special Events Manager*

Kay Payne, *Sales Manager*

Becky Allred
Heather Drew
Annie Feltus
Nancy Gardner
Donna Helms
Jamie Huffman Jones
JoJo Kittell
Samaria Mascagni
Nicole McCain
Erica Parker
Tiffany Robinson
Katherine Shell
Marian Steward
Christine Millner
Julie Tabor
Catherine Tapp
Lynette Vinson
Tiffany Warriner

Lisa Baxter, *Sustainer Advisor*

Cindy Miller, *Sustainer Advisor*

Susan Reynolds, *Sustainer Advisor*

Acknowledgments

By Invitation Only

Catering to You

Cranford Johnson Robinson and Woods

Fifth Season

Foster Cochran

Full Moon

Lee Edwards

Little Rock Convention & Visitors Bureau

Little Rock School District

Ron Robinson

Secretary of State Charlie Daniels

Food Photographer: Ron Manville
Ron is a culinary, travel, and lifestyle photographer. He is the chief food photographer for Johnson and Wales University, ACF Culinary Olympic Team and Grace Ormonde's *Wedding Style* magazine. He has shot thirty-five cookbooks, including two James Beard and IACP winners and two Tabasco award winners. His works also include three books for Chef John Folse and *Wolfgang Makes It Easy* by Chef Wolfgang Puck. Ron was born and raised in Virginia and currently lives in Nashville, Tennessee.

Food Stylist: Mary Ann Fowlkes

Appetizers &
Beverages

A Taste from Downtown

Downtown Little Rock

Downtown Little Rock brings together a taste of the past, present, and future. Since our city became the Territorial Capital of Arkansas in 1821, the prosperity of the Natural State has been instrumentally linked to the vitality and diversity of downtown Little Rock. Our heritage is captured in sites like the Quapaw Quarter, the Old State House, the State Capitol, the Historic Arkansas Museum, and MacArthur Park. Our commerce is tied to the dozens of businesses located in world-class facilities, such as Stephens Inc., one of the largest investment firms in America not headquartered on Wall Street. Our travel and tourism is keyed to the Little Rock Convention Center, and our cultural life is anchored to the arts, museums, theaters, and libraries in the downtown area. Feel the pulse as you experience our "uptown" downtown.

Ceviche

8	ounces shrimp, peeled and deveined	1/2	red onion, finely chopped
8	ounces snapper or flounder, cut into 1-inch pieces	1	tablespoon chopped fresh cilantro
2	jalapeño chiles, seeded and finely chopped		Grated zest of 1 lime
	Juice of 8 limes		Salt and freshly ground pepper to taste
1	vine-ripened tomato, chopped		Lime wedges and chopped fresh cilantro, for garnish

Combine the shrimp, fish and jalapeño chiles in a bowl. Add the lime juice and toss to coat well. Marinate, covered, in the refrigerator for 6 hours or longer, tossing occasionally. Add the tomato, onion, 1 tablespoon chopped cilantro, the lime zest, salt and pepper at serving time and mix gently. Spoon into martini glasses and garnish each with a lime wedge and additional chopped cilantro.

SERVES 4 TO 6

Chipotle Grilled Shrimp Relish with Potato Crisps

Donnie Ferneau, *Chef/Owner of Ferneau*

1	pound shrimp, peeled and deveined	1	bunch cilantro, finely chopped
1/3	cup hickory-flavor chipotle sauce	2	garlic cloves, minced
1	large red onion, chopped		Juice of 1 lime
8	ounces frozen corn kernels		Salt and pepper to taste
1	large red bell pepper, finely chopped	2	pounds kettle-cooked potato chips

Toss the shrimp and chipotle sauce in a bowl. Grill the shrimp until done to taste. Cool to room temperature. Chop into 1/4-inch pieces. Combine the onion, corn, red bell pepper, cilantro, garlic and lime juice in a large mixing bowl and mix well. Fold in the shrimp. Season with salt and pepper. Chill, covered, in the refrigerator for 15 minutes to blend the flavors. Spoon into small bowls or martini glasses to serve. Serve with the chips.

SERVES 8

La Petit Roche

Our city can trace its roots to an actual "little rock" first observed by early explorers. The French used the designation of "la petit roche" to describe this first major rock outcropping when traveling from the Gulf of Mexico up the Mississippi and Arkansas Rivers. This landmark became widely used by pioneering river traffickers and was a well-known river crossing. You, too, can discover this anchoring point. It's located on the bank of the Arkansas River at the south pier of the Union Pacific Railroad Bridge at the approximate mid-point of Riverfront Park.

Caramelized Green Chile Calamari and Lump Crab Tapas

Michael Selig, *Executive Chef/Owner of Vermillion*

1	jalapeño chile, chopped	6	ounces steamed lump crab meat
2	ounces fresh or canned corn kernels	1	tablespoon chopped red onion
1	tablespoon brown sugar	2	tablespoons chopped red bell
3/4	cup Southwestern Marinade (below)		pepper
			Crostini toast points
6	ounces calamari, sliced into 1/2-inch rings		Cilantro sprigs, for garnish

Oil a sauté pan or spray with nonstick cooking spray. Heat over medium heat and add the jalapeño chile. Sauté until tender. Remove from the heat and add the corn and brown sugar. Cook over medium heat until the corn is tender.

Add the Southwestern Marinade and bring to a boil. Remove from the heat and stir in the calamari. Cover and let steep for 2 minutes or until the calamari are opaque.

Chill the mixture in the freezer for 1 minute. Add the crab meat, onion and red bell pepper; toss to mix well. Serve on crostini and garnish with sprigs of cilantro. You can also serve with chips as a dip.

SERVES 6

Southwestern Marinade

1 1/2	tablespoons chopped chipotle chiles
2	tablespoons chopped cilantro
1	tablespoon honey
1/4	cup Dijon mustard
1 1/2	cups orange juice
1	tablespoon cumin

Combine the chipotle chiles, cilantro, honey, Dijon mustard, orange juice and cumin in a blender and process until puréed.

MAKES 2 CUPS

Warm Lemon-Herbed Olives

1   pint (2 cups) mixed olives in brine
1 to 2 tablespoons Lemon Olive Oil (see below)
    Grated zest of 1 lemon
2   tablespoons mixed minced fresh thyme,
    rosemary and oregano

Bring the olives and the brine just to a simmer in a saucepan and cook until heated through. Drain the olives and combine with the Lemon Olive Oil in a bowl. Add the lemon zest and fresh herbs; toss to mix well. Serve warm.

You can store the olives in the refrigerator for weeks and reheat briefly in the microwave.

SERVES 8

Photograph on page 19.

Blue Cheese Puffs

16   ounces cream cheese, softened
4   ounces blue cheese, crumbled
1   cup mayonnaise
1   tablespoon grated onion

1/4 cup fresh chives, chopped
1/2 teaspoon cayenne pepper
2   loaves very thinly sliced bread
     Paprika to taste

Combine the cream cheese, blue cheese and mayonnaise in a blender and process until smooth. Mix with the onion, chives and cayenne pepper in a bowl.

Cut the bread into small circles with a shot glass or small cutter. Place on a baking sheet. Spoon about 1 teaspoon of the cheese mixture onto each circle. Sprinkle with paprika. Bake at 350 degrees for 15 minutes. Serve warm.

SERVES 14 TO 16

Lemon Olive Oil

To make Lemon Olive Oil, combine one cup of olive oil with the grated zest of two lemons. Let stand for two hours at room temperature and then pour through a sieve, if desired. Use in pasta dishes or salads to brighten up the flavor.

Rooftop Cocktails

Basil Lemon Drop Martinis

38

Warm Lemon-Herbed Olives

16

Artichokes with Lemon Aïoli

18

Blue Cheese Puffs

16

Pot Stickers with Wasabi Plum Sauce

29

Crab Cakes with Mango Papaya Salsa

32

Peppercorn Beef Tenderloin

77

Refrigerator Rolls

199

Grasshopper Tartlets

225

Wine: Pinot Noir

Artichokes with Lemon Aïoli

1	cup sour cream
	Juice and some pulp of 1 or 2 lemons
	Grated zest of 1/2 lemon
1 to	2 teaspoons minced garlic
1/4	teaspoon cayenne pepper, or to taste
	Kosher salt and pepper to taste
4	globe artichokes
	Juice of 1 lemon

Combine the sour cream with the juice and some of the pulp of one or two lemons in a mixing bowl for the lemon aïoli. Add the lemon zest, garlic and cayenne pepper. Season with kosher salt and pepper. Chill, covered, in the refrigerator.

Trim the prickly tip of each artichoke leaf with kitchen shears. Leave the stems to use as handles. Rub the artichokes with the juice of one lemon. Place the artichokes stem ends up in a steamer basket over boiling water. Steam for 30 to 45 minutes or until the artichoke bottoms are tender when pierced with a sharp knife, checking occasionally to maintain the level of water. You can also steam for 30 minutes and hold, covered, for 15 minutes. Drain the artichokes and serve warm or chilled with the lemon aïoli.

SERVES 4

River Market

Every visitor to Little Rock needs to include the River Market District in his travel itinerary. Located downtown along the Arkansas River, this area is virtually exploding with entertainment, restaurants, education, and fun. At its heart is the Ottenheimer Market Hall, housing a number of year-round merchants featuring fare from bakery goods to international cuisine along with seasonal activities, such as a farmers' market for produce and ice skating in the winter. For more fun, amble over to the Main Branch of the Central Arkansas Library System or tour the magic of the Museum of Discovery. Ready, set, go!

Chicken Salad Appetizer

4	cups shredded cooked chicken		1	cup mayonnaise
1	rib celery, chopped		1	teaspoon Dijon mustard
4	green onions, thinly sliced		2	teaspoons fresh lemon juice
1/4	cup chopped oil-packed			Salt and freshly ground pepper
	sun-dried tomatoes, drained			to taste
2	tablespoons chopped pecans			Fresh spinach
2	tablespoons finely chopped parsley			Water crackers
1 1/2	teaspoons finely chopped			
	fresh dill			

Combine the chicken, celery, green onions, sun-dried tomatoes, pecans, parsley and dill in a mixing bowl and mix well. Whisk the mayonnaise, Dijon mustard, lemon juice, salt and pepper together in a small bowl. Add to the chicken mixture and mix well. Chill until serving time.

Place one spinach leaf on each water cracker and top with 1 tablespoon of the chicken salad. Arrange on a platter.

This chicken salad can also be used as a sandwich filling or scooped onto lettuce leaves and served with assorted fruit, sliced tomatoes and sliced avocados.

SERVES 8

Crostini with Goat Cheese and Walnuts

4	ounces goat cheese		1	tablespoon chopped
1	baguette, sliced and toasted			fresh rosemary
3/4	cup chopped walnuts, toasted			Honey to taste

Spread the goat cheese on the toasted baguette slices. Sprinkle with the walnuts and rosemary. Drizzle lightly with honey. Serve at room temperature.

SERVES 8

Peperonata

3   tablespoons extra-virgin olive oil
2   large red bell peppers, chopped
2   large yellow bell peppers, chopped
1   onion, chopped
2 or 3 garlic cloves, thinly sliced
2   tablespoons red wine vinegar
1   tablespoon chopped fresh Italian parsley
2   tablespoons capers, drained
     Salt and red pepper flakes to taste
     Goat cheese, softened
     Toasted 1/4-inch baguette slices or melba toast rounds

Heat the olive oil in a large heavy skillet over high heat until very hot. Add the red bell peppers, yellow bell peppers and onion and sauté until light brown. Reduce the heat to medium and add the garlic. Cook, covered, for 10 to 20 minutes or until the bell peppers are tender.

Increase the heat and stir in the vinegar. Cook for 3 minutes or until the vinegar evaporates, stirring constantly. Remove from the heat and stir in the parsley and capers. Season with salt and red pepper flakes.

Spread goat cheese on toasted baguette slices and top with the peperonata. You can also present the peperonata on a tray with goat cheese, baguette slices and a spreader and allow guests to assemble it themselves. Combine the peperonata with goat cheese and pesto for a sandwich filling or serve as an accompaniment for meat.

SERVES 12

Photograph on page 19.

Julius Breckling Riverfront Park

*Stretching along the Arkansas River in downtown Little Rock is Riverfront Park.
A sanctuary for relaxation and a beehive of community activity, the park has an array of walking paths and benches, a pleasure boat wharf, a belvedere, a three-tiered fountain, and
a unique permanent "tent" for riverside entertainment. Enjoy a free outdoor movie in the summertime.
Cheer the fireworks and Arkansas Symphony concert on the Fourth of July. Relish the
sights and sounds of Riverfest weekend, Little Rock's biggest springtime festival. Or just "cool it"
and soak in the calm of watching one of America's grand rivers roll on by.*

Baked Artichoke and Corn Dip

1 (14-ounce) can artichoke hearts, drained and chopped	1 cup (4 ounces) shredded Cheddar cheese
1 (16-ounce) can corn kernels, drained	1 cup (4 ounces) grated Parmesan cheese
1/2 cup chopped green onions	1/2 cup mayonnaise
1/2 to 1 (4-ounce) can chopped jalapeño chiles, drained	1/2 teaspoon garlic salt

Combine the artichoke hearts, corn, green onions, jalapeño chiles, Cheddar cheese and Parmesan cheese in a bowl. Add the mayonnaise and garlic salt and mix well. Spoon into a lightly greased baking dish. Bake at 350 degrees for 20 minutes. Serve with corn chips.

You can substitute fresh garlic for the garlic salt and fresh jalapeño chiles for the canned chiles if preferred.

SERVES 12

Black-Eyed Pea Dip

4 jalapeño chiles, chopped	3 (16-ounce) cans black-eyed peas, drained
1 small onion, finely chopped	
1 cup (2 sticks) butter	3 dashes of hot sauce
2 garlic cloves, minced	Salt and coarse pepper to taste
1 teaspoon ground cumin	2 cups (8 ounces) shredded sharp Cheddar cheese
1 teaspoon ground coriander	

Sauté the jalapeño chiles and onion in 1/2 cup of the butter in a saucepan until the onion is translucent. Add the remaining 1/2 cup butter and the garlic, cumin and coriander. Cook until the butter melts. Add two cans of the peas and mash with a potato masher. Stir in the remaining can of peas, the hot sauce, salt and pepper. Add the cheese and heat until the cheese melts, stirring to mix well. Serve hot with corn bread or corn chips.

SERVES 8

The Capital Hotel

Mere words are hardly adequate to describe the elegance and luxury of one of America's premier retreats—The Capital Hotel at Markham and Louisiana Streets in downtown Little Rock. Originally opened in the 1870s, this structure with its iron façade—one of the few such buildings in the world—and its white marble charm has undergone numerous renovations, including a $25 million "rebirth" completed in 2007. Make sure that you see the hotel's enormous elevator, complete with seating. History has it that President U.S. Grant used the elevator for himself and his horse during a post–Civil War visit. From its upscale rooms to its relaxing bar to the classic dining room, this landmark hotel says "world-class" wherever you turn!

Spicy Pimento Cheese Spread

3   ounces cream cheese, softened
1¹/2 cups (6 ounces) shredded
     Cheddar cheese
1   cup (4 ounces) shredded
     Monterey Jack cheese
1   (2-ounce) jar chopped pimento
1   poblano chile, seeded and minced
1   (4-ounce) can chopped
     green chiles

2   teaspoons grated onion
2   garlic cloves, minced
1/4 to 1/2 cup toasted chopped pecans
     (optional)
1/2 cup mayonnaise
2   teaspoons Worcestershire sauce
2   dashes of hot sauce

Combine the cream cheese, Cheddar cheese and Monterey Jack cheese in a large bowl. Add the pimento, poblano chile, green chiles, onion, garlic and pecans and mix well. Stir in the mayonnaise, Worcestershire sauce and hot sauce. Serve with baguette slices as a spread, with crudités as a dip or as the filling for grilled or ungrilled sandwiches.

SERVES 10

Goat Cheese Mousse

Peter Brave, *Chef/Owner of Brave New Restaurant*

8   ounces cream cheese, softened
8   ounces goat cheese, softened
5   eggs
1¹/4 cups heavy cream
1   teaspoon Tabasco sauce

Process the cream cheese, goat cheese, eggs, cream and Tabasco sauce in a food processor until smooth. Spoon into eight buttered and floured baking ramekins. Place in a baking pan and add enough water to the pan to reach halfway up the sides of the ramekins. Bake at 350 degrees for 45 minutes. Serve warm with water crackers and fruit. This is also good to serve as a side dish with meat.

SERVES 8

Crawfish Dip

2	tablespoons butter	1	teaspoon cayenne pepper
1	bunch green onions, chopped	1 1/2	cups (6 ounces) shredded white
2	tablespoons all-purpose flour		American cheese
1/2	cup heavy cream	3	ounces (3/4 cup) shredded
1/4	cup white wine		Swiss cheese
1/4	teaspoon garlic powder	1	pound crawfish, cooked
1	teaspoon salt		and peeled

Combine the butter and green onions in a microwave-safe bowl. Microwave on High for 3 minutes. Add the flour, cream, wine, garlic powder, salt and cayenne pepper and mix well. Microwave on High for 1 to 2 minutes. Stir in the American cheese, Swiss cheese and crawfish. Microwave for 6 minutes longer. Stir before serving.

SERVES 8

Roasted Red Pepper Hummus

1	(15-ounce) can garbanzo beans, drained	2	tablespoons warm water
1 1/2	large red bell peppers, roasted (about three 3×6-inch pieces)	3	tablespoons olive oil
			Granted zest of 1/2 lemon
	Juice of 1 lemon	3/4	teaspoon cumin
1/2	cup coarsely chopped parsley	3/4	teaspoon salt
2	garlic cloves, chopped	1/4	teaspoon cayenne pepper, or to taste
3	tablespoons tahini		

Place the garbanzo beans, red bell peppers, lemon juice, parsley and garlic in a small food processor. Add the tahini, water, olive oil, lemon zest, cumin, salt and cayenne pepper and pulse until smooth. Adjust the seasoning. Chill for 8 hours or longer to blend flavors. Serve as a dip with fresh vegetables, pita bread or crackers. This can be stored, covered, in the refrigerator for up to 1 week.

SERVES 6

War Memorial Tailgate

Mother-in-Law Mix

40

Crawfish Dip

24

Mahogany Chicken Wings

30

Spicy Nuts

35

Beef Brisket

78

Apple Sandwiches

170

Brewery Bread

190

Iced Sugar Cookies

218

Wine: Moscato d'Asti

Salmon Torta

1	cup (2 sticks) butter, softened	2	tablespoons minced purple onion
16	ounces cream cheese, softened	3	tablespoons capers, drained
4	ounces smoked salmon		Capers and fresh dill, for garnish
2	tablespoons chopped fresh dill		

Cream the butter and cream cheese in a mixing bowl until light. Press one-third of the mixture onto the bottom of a lightly greased 6-inch springform pan. Layer the salmon, chopped dill, onion, capers and remaining cream cheese mixture one-half at a time in the prepared pan.

Chill in the refrigerator until set. Unmold onto a serving plate and garnish with additional capers and dill. Serve with bagel crisps or crackers.

SERVES 8

Spinach and Feta Cheese Pizza

1	prepared pizza crust	1 1/4	cups (5 ounces) crumbled
1	tablespoon olive oil		feta cheese
1	bunch baby spinach leaves	1	(4-ounce) can sliced black olives
1	tomato, sliced	1/4	cup (1 ounce) shredded
1	red onion, sliced, or to taste		Parmesan cheese

Place the pizza crust on a baking sheet and drizzle with the olive oil. Layer the spinach, tomato and onion on the crust. Top with the feta cheese, black olives and Parmesan cheese. Bake at 350 degrees for 20 minutes or until the crust is brown. Cut into wedges to serve.

SERVES 8

The Peabody Ducks

The most famous ducks in Arkansas capture smiles daily in downtown Little Rock at the Peabody Hotel. In the fall of 2000, Peabody Hotel Group embarked on a $40 million renovation of the former Excelsior Hotel and incorporated this trademark tradition. The Peabody Ducks leave their Royal Peabody Duck Palace promptly at 11:00 a.m. sharp and are greeted by red carpet service in the hotel lobby. They are accompanied daily by the Duck Master—in a red- and gold-trimmed jacket with a brass-head duck cane. As the "King Cotton March" plays, the Peabody Ducks meander down the carpet, ascend three steps, and dive into the fountain. They enjoy frolicking in the lobby until 5:00 p.m. and then quickly return to their royal residence upstairs. Lucky ducks, indeed!

Spicy Brie Tarts

2   jalapeño chiles, seeded and minced
1   tablespoon butter
2   tablespoons cider vinegar
1   (12-ounce) jar raspberry preserves
20   slices white bread
1   (10-ounce) wheel Brie cheese, chopped
     Chopped fresh chives, for garnish

Sauté the jalapeño chiles in the butter in a small saucepan until tender. Add the cider vinegar and preserves and mix well. Bring to a simmer and cook for 5 minutes, stirring to prevent scorching.

Roll the bread very flat and cut into rounds with a fluted 3-inch cutter. Press the rounds into greased muffin cups. Bake at 350 degrees for 8 to 10 minutes or until toasted. Cool completely. Reduce the oven temperature to 300 degrees.

Fill the bread cups with the Brie cheese and top each with 1/2 teaspoon or more of the preserves mixture. Bake at 300 degrees for 10 minutes or until the cheese melts. Garnish with chopped chives.

SERVES 20

Baked Brie

Baked Brie is a quick and easy appetizer that pleases a crowd. Simply cut a piece of puff pastry dough large enough to completely wrap around the Brie you have chosen. Place the puff pastry flat on a work surface. Brush the edges with egg wash. Place the Brie in the center of the dough and top with two tablespoons of your favorite jam or jelly. Bring the sides of the pastry up to cover the Brie, tucking in any extra to create a pleasing fold. Bake at 350 degrees until golden brown and serve hot with sliced green apples and crackers.

Razorback Meatballs

1	pound cooked ham	1	tablespoon mustard
1	pound ground pork	1/2	cup water
1	cup milk	1/2	cup vinegar
2	slices bread, crumbled	1	cup packed brown sugar
3	green onions, chopped	2	teaspoons mustard
2	tablespoons chopped parsley		

Process the ham in a food processor until very finely chopped. Combine with the pork, milk, bread, green onions, parsley and 1 tablespoon mustard in a large bowl and mix just until combined; do not overmix. Shape into 1- to 1 1/2-inch balls. Place in a greased baking dish.

Combine the water, vinegar, brown sugar and 2 teaspoons mustard in a saucepan. Bring to a simmer over medium heat. Pour over the meatballs. Bake at 300 degrees for 1 hour and 10 minutes.

SERVES 10 TO 12

Stuffed Mushrooms

3	hot Italian sausages, casings removed and sausage crumbled	1/2	teaspoon Worcestershire sauce
			Salt and pepper to taste
1 1/2	teaspoons dried oregano	1	egg yolk
2	small garlic cloves, minced	24	large mushroom caps
1/2	cup (2 ounces) grated Parmesan cheese	1/3	cup dry white wine
8	ounces cream cheese, softened	1/2	cup (2 ounces) grated Parmesan cheese

Sauté the sausage with the oregano in a large heavy skillet over medium heat, stirring until the sausage is brown and crumbly. Add the garlic and sauté for 1 minute. Remove to a large bowl with a slotted spoon and cool. Stir in 1/2 cup Parmesan cheese, the cream cheese and Worcestershire sauce. Season with salt and pepper. Add the egg yolk and mix well.

Brush the cavity of each mushroom cap with the wine. Spoon 1 tablespoon of the sausage mixture into each mushroom cap and sprinkle with 1/2 cup Parmesan cheese. Arrange filling side up in a 10×15-inch baking dish brushed with olive oil. Bake at 350 degrees for 25 minutes or until the mushroom caps are tender and the filling is brown. Serve immediately or store in the refrigerator for up to 24 hours before serving.

SERVES 24

Pot Stickers with Wasabi Plum Sauce

1	pound hot pork sausage	30	won ton wrappers
2	green onions, finely chopped		Cabbage leaves
1	teaspoon minced fresh ginger	1/4	cup plum sauce
2	tablespoons hoisin sauce	1/4	cup light soy sauce
1	tablespoon chili garlic sauce		Grated fresh wasabi or wasabi
1	tablespoon light soy sauce		powder to taste

Combine the sausage, green onions, ginger, hoisin sauce, chili garlic sauce and 1 tablespoon soy sauce in a bowl and mix well. Arrange the won ton wrappers on a dry work surface, working in batches. Brush the edges of the wrappers with water. Place 1 tablespoon of the sausage mixture on each wrapper and fold the wrapper over to enclose the filling; press the edges to seal.

Pour 1/2 to 1 inch of water into a large saucepan and place a metal steamer rack in the saucepan; the level of the water should not reach the bottom of the steamer rack. Line the steamer rack with cabbage leaves and bring the water to a boil.

Arrange a single layer of dumplings in the steamer rack with the sides not touching. Steam for 8 minutes or until the dumplings are cooked through; remove to a warm bowl. Repeat the process with the remaining dumplings, adding additional water and replacing the cabbage leaves as necessary.

Whisk the plum sauce and 1/4 cup soy sauce together in a small saucepan. Cook until heated through. Stir in the wasabi. Serve with the pot stickers.

SERVES 12

Mount Holly Cemetery

*Located on Broadway near Interstate 630, Mount Holly Cemetery has often been called
"The Westminster Abbey of Arkansas" because it is the final resting place
of so many notable Arkansans. This four-square-block landmark established in 1843 is
listed on the National Register of Historic Places and is one of the most memorable
Victorian cemeteries in the United States. Its quaint bell house sits in the middle of the cemetery
at a point that once was the highest in Little Rock. Looking in any direction, you
will find the past leaders of Arkansas—governors, senators, justices, and many more—
along with monuments that vary from classical to creative in style.
Here's your opportunity to walk among the ages.
"When I was a young reporter, I used to steal away every few weeks for some quiet
time in Mount Holly Cemetery. There, whatever news seemed so urgent
outside those black iron gates felt elegantly, serenely passé. It was a fine place for regaining
perspective. I visited in all seasons, but my favorite month was May, when the
gracious mulberry tree that shaded the Pike family graves threw a party for birds with its
fruit. I'd bring a basket. My children were born in May, and for years we celebrated
their birthdays with bowls of cake and ice cream—topped with juicy black mulberries."*

—Mara Leveritt, author and reporter

Thai Barbecued Chicken Satay

1	cup peanut butter	2	dashes of Tabasco sauce
1	cup soy sauce	2	cups cilantro, chopped
1/2	cup honey	8	green onions, chopped
1/4	cup sesame oil	6	garlic cloves, crushed
2	tablespoons olive oil	1 3/4	pounds chicken tenders

*C*ombine the peanut butter, soy sauce, honey, sesame oil, olive oil and Tabasco sauce in a bowl and mix well. Stir in the cilantro, green onions and garlic. Spoon half the mixture into a saucepan and reserve.

Add the chicken tenders to the remaining sauce in the bowl and stir to coat evenly. Thread the chicken onto skewers and let stand for 5 minutes. Grill for 3 to 5 minutes on each side or until cooked through. Heat the reserved sauce until heated through. Serve with the chicken skewers.

SERVES 6

Mahogany Chicken Wings

1 1/2	cups soy sauce	3/4	cup cider vinegar
1	cup plus 2 tablespoons hoisin sauce	1/2	cup honey
		18	green onions, minced
3/4	cup plum sauce	6	large garlic cloves, minced
3/4	cup dry sherry	24	chicken wings

*M*ix the soy sauce, hoisin sauce, plum sauce, sherry, vinegar, honey, green onions and garlic in a medium saucepan. Bring to a boil and reduce the heat. Simmer for 5 minutes. Cool to room temperature.

Combine the sauce with the chicken in a large bowl and mix well. Marinate in the refrigerator for 8 hours or longer. Drain the chicken, reserving the marinade.

Arrange the chicken in two large shallow baking pans. Bake at 350 degrees for 1 to 1 1/2 hours, basting every 20 minutes with the reserved marinade and turning occasionally to brown evenly; switch the pans half-way through the cooking time.

Cool the chicken on a foil-lined tray and store in the refrigerator for up to 3 days. Serve at room temperature.

SERVES 12

Chafing Dish Ducks

4	ducks, cleaned	1	apple, cut into quarters
	Buttermilk	1	onion, cut into quarters
1/4	cup Worcestershire sauce	4	ribs celery, cut into quarters
	Salt and pepper to taste	1	cup red wine

Combine the ducks with enough buttermilk to cover in a large bowl and let stand for 1 hour. Drain and rinse the ducks. Season with Worcestershire sauce, salt and pepper. Stuff the ducks with the apple, onion and celery. Place in a large roasting pan and add the wine.

Roast at 350 degrees for 2 1/2 hours or until the ducks are very tender, basting frequently with the pan drippings. Remove the ducks to a platter and let cool.

Shred the duck meat, discarding the skin and bones. Combine with the pan drippings in a chafing dish. Serve with party rolls.

SERVES 8 TO 10

Baked Oysters

1	small onion, chopped	2	cups fresh oysters
2	garlic cloves, minced	1/4	cup bread crumbs
3	tablespoons butter	1/4	cup (1 ounce) grated
8	ounces mushrooms, sliced		Parmesan cheese
1/2	cup white wine	3	tablespoons melted butter
16	ounces fresh spinach		Fresh lemon juice
	Salt and pepper to taste		Toasted bread points

Sauté the onion and garlic in 3 tablespoons butter in a large sauté pan. Add the mushrooms and wine and cook for 3 minutes or until the mushrooms are tender. Add the spinach and cook until the spinach is wilted. Season with salt and pepper.

Add the oysters and cook just until heated through. Spoon the mixture into lightly greased muffin cups, placing one oyster in each cup. Mix the bread crumbs and cheese in a small bowl and sprinkle over the tops. Drizzle with the melted butter.

Bake at 350 degrees for 20 minutes or until the tops begin to brown. Squeeze lemon juice over the tops. Remove carefully from the muffin cups and place on toasted bread points. You can also prepare this in oyster half-shells.

SERVES 8

Crab Cakes with Mango Papaya Salsa

MANGO PAPAYA SALSA

2	cups finely chopped mangoes
2	cups finely chopped papayas
1	large red bell pepper, chopped
1	onion, chopped
1	cup water
1/2	cup sugar
1/2	cup cider vinegar
4	dashes of Tabasco sauce
1	teaspoon ground ginger
1	teaspoon allspice
1/4	teaspoon salt

CRAB CAKES

1	pound crab meat
1	egg
1/2	cup bread crumbs
1/4	cup mayonnaise
1	tablespoon chopped cilantro
1/4	teaspoon Tabasco sauce
1/2	teaspoon cumin
1/4	teaspoon white pepper
2	tablespoons butter

Place the mangoes, papayas, red bell pepper and onion in a small saucepan. Add the water, sugar, vinegar, Tabasco sauce, ginger, allspice and salt. Cook over medium-low heat for 30 minutes or until the mangoes are tender and the mixture is reduced to the desired consistency.

Combine the crab meat, egg, bread crumbs, mayonnaise, cilantro, Tabasco sauce, cumin and white pepper in a bowl and mix well. Shape into 1 1/4-inch cakes. Sauté in the butter in a sauté pan for 3 minutes on each side or until golden brown and cooked through. Serve with the salsa.

SERVES 8

Cutting a Mango

Mangoes have a large flat pit in the center that can be difficult to navigate when chopping. To retrieve the most fruit, place the mango so that the stem is pointing toward you. Cut lengthwise about one inch on either side of the stem, cutting as close to the pit as possible. Trim away any excess fruit from the pit and chop. Score the cut sides of the two halves of the mango and turn inside out. Carefully cut the protruding mango cubes from the peel.

Scallops Rockefeller

Antoine Seyer, *Executive Chef/Owner of Gypsy*

^{1}/2 onion, coarsely chopped	1 teaspoon chopped fresh tarragon,
3 ribs celery, coarsely chopped	or ^{1}/3 teaspoon dried tarragon
^{1}/2 bunch green onions,	1 teaspoon Pernod
coarsely chopped	1 cup Besciamella Sauce (page 95)
^{1}/2 cup (1 stick) butter	1 cup bread crumbs (preferably fresh)
1 (10-ounce) package frozen	Pinch of cayenne pepper
chopped spinach, cooked	Salt and black pepper to taste
and drained	24 to 30 fresh scallops
^{1}/2 bunch parsley, trimmed	^{1}/2 cup (about) béarnaise sauce
and chopped	(optional)

Sauté the onion, celery and green onions in the butter in a skillet until tender. Add the spinach, parsley, tarragon and Pernod and cook until heated through. Stir in the Besciamella Sauce and bread crumbs. Season with cayenne pepper, salt and black pepper. The spinach mixture should not be too dry or too moist.

Arrange the scallops in a single layer in a lightly buttered gratin dish. Top each scallop with a spoonful of the spinach mixture. Bake at 400 degrees for 15 minutes. Just before serving, top each scallop with 1 teaspoon of the béarnaise sauce. Broil for 5 to 10 seconds or until heated through.

SERVES 6

Ginger Lime Shrimp

2 large shallots, chopped	1^1/2 tablespoons sugar
4 garlic cloves, minced	^{1}/4 cup chopped green onions
2 tablespoons chopped fresh ginger	^{1}/4 cup peanut oil or olive oil
^{3}/4 cup soy sauce	^{1}/4 teaspoon freshly ground pepper
^{1}/2 cup fresh lime juice	2 pounds large shrimp, peeled
2 tablespoons honey	and deveined

Combine the shallots, garlic, ginger, soy sauce, lime juice, honey and sugar in a blender and process until smooth. Add the green onions and peanut oil and process to blend well. Season with pepper.

Thread the shrimp onto wooden skewers. Combine with the ginger mixture in a shallow dish. Marinate at room temperature for 20 to 60 minutes.

Preheat a grill to high. Drain the skewers and grill for 2 to 3 minutes on each side or until cooked through.

SERVES 8

Shrimp Bread

1   (10-ounce) loaf French bread
1   cup chopped onion
1/2 cup chopped celery
2   tablespoons minced garlic
2   tablespoons butter
1   pound shrimp, peeled
1/4 cup Old Bay seasoning
1/2 teaspoon crab boil
1/3 cup chopped green onions
2   cups heavy cream
1   cup (4 ounces) shredded mozzarella cheese

Cut the bread into halves lengthwise. Hollow out the halves, reserving the bread removed and the intact shells. Crumble enough of the reserved bread to measure 1/2 cup. Place the bread shells cut side up on a baking sheet.

Sauté the onion, celery and garlic in the butter in a sauté pan until the onion is translucent. Add the shrimp, Old Bay seasoning and crab boil and simmer for 3 to 4 minutes or until the shrimp are cooked through. Add the green onions and crumble in the reserved 1/2 cup bread. Stir in the cream. Spoon the mixture into the bread shells.

Sprinkle with the cheese. Bake at 350 degrees for 10 minutes or until the cheese melts. Let stand for 5 minutes. Cut into pieces to serve as an appetizer or into halves to serve with a green salad as a main dish.

SERVES 8 AS AN APPETIZER OR 4 AS A MAIN DISH

The Villa Marre

Take a drive by 1321 South Scott Street in the Quapaw Quarter District and you'll see one of the most elegant and fashionable houses built in the 1880s—the Villa Marre. Combining Italianate and Second Empire architecture, this home was created by Angelo and Jennie Marre and over the years has been the residence of a number of families, a nursing home, a dance studio, and even a boardinghouse. The restored structure took a starring role on national television when it was shown weekly on the opening of the comedy series, Designing Women. Since 2002, the Villa Marre has been returned to its original role as a private residence, while continuing to serve as a reminder of Southern grace and charm.

Spicy Nuts

2 tablespoons vegetable oil
2 teaspoons Worcestershire sauce
1^1/$_2$ teaspoons chili powder
^{1}/$_2$ teaspoon garlic salt
^{1}/$_4$ teaspoon cayenne pepper
1^1/$_2$ cups cashews
1^1/$_2$ cups peanuts

*C*ombine the oil with the Worcestershire sauce, chili powder, garlic salt and cayenne pepper in a large bowl. Add the cashews and peanuts and toss to coat evenly. Spread evenly in a 9×13-inch baking dish. Bake at 300 degrees for 20 minutes, stirring once or twice.

SERVES 12

Berry Iced Tea

8 cups water
2 tablespoons lemon juice
^{1}/$_2$ cup sugar
8 raspberry tea bags
2 cups cranberry juice
   Lemon slices, for garnish

*B*ring the water to a boil in a large saucepan. Remove from the heat and add the lemon juice and sugar, stirring to dissolve the sugar completely. Add the tea bags and cranberry juice and steep for 10 minutes. Remove the tea bags. Cool the tea to room temperature. Store in the refrigerator. Serve over ice and garnish with lemon slices.

For a refreshing summer cocktail, add 1 to 2 cups raspberry-flavor vodka to the tea.

MAKES 10 CUPS

Poinsettia Cocktail

2 ounces (1/4 cup) cranberry juice
4 ounces (1/2 cup) Champagne
1/2 ounce (1 tablespoon) Triple Sec
    Ice
    Cranberry skewers, for garnish
    Sugar, for garnish

Combine the cranberry juice, Champagne and Triple Sec with ice in a cocktail shaker. Shake well and strain into a Champagne flute or martini glass. Thread fresh cranberries onto a skewer, dip into water and roll in sugar to serve as a garnish.

SERVES 1

Raspberry Mojitos

1 cup fresh raspberries
1/3 cup sugar
12 mint leaves
    Juice of 1/2 lime
8 teaspoons sugar
1/4 cup light rum

    Crushed ice
4 splashes of club soda
    Fresh raspberries, thin lime
    wedges and mint leaves,
    for garnish

Bring 1 cup raspberries and 1/3 cup sugar to a boil in a small saucepan. Cook for 10 minutes, stirring occasionally. Press through a strainer to remove the seeds.

Place three mint leaves, one-fourth of the lime juice and 2 teaspoons sugar in each of four glasses; crush the mint with a spoon. Add 1 tablespoon of the rum and 1 tablespoon of the raspberry syrup to each glass and mix well. Add crushed ice and a splash of club soda to each and stir to mix. Garnish with skewered fresh raspberries, lime wedges and additional mint leaves.

SERVES 4

Holiday Brew

Combine two cups each of pineapple juice, apple juice, and water in a saucepan.
Add the rind of one orange, one cinnamon stick, one teaspoon of cloves,
one teaspoon of allspice, one piece of ginger, and one vanilla bean. Simmer over low heat and
fill your home with a wonderful holiday scent. This is not meant for consumption.

Basil Lemon Drop Martini

Lee Edwards, *President of Lee Edwards Distributing*

Water
Sugar
Fresh lime juice
Fresh lemon juice
Ice
Basil leaves
Citrus vodka
Curls of lemon zest, for garnish

Make a simple syrup by bringing water to a boil in a saucepan and adding an equal amount of sugar, stirring to dissolve the sugar completely. Boil for 1 to 2 minutes. Cool to room temperature. Mix two parts of lime juice and one part of lemon juice in a cup. Combine two parts of this juice mixture with one part of the syrup for a sweet-and-sour mixture.

Fill a 2-cup mixing glass with straight sides half full of ice. Add six to eight basil leaves. Place the flat end of a good-quality muddler in the glass and hold with one hand. Cover the glass with the other hand, leaving a narrow opening between the thumb and index finger for the muddler. Muddle the basil until it is torn up but not long enough to melt the ice.

Add a three- to four-count measure of vodka to the mixing glass, adjusting to individual taste. Stir in twice as much of the sweet-and-sour mixture as you did vodka. Pour into a tall metal shaker and fit the glass tightly over the top. Shake up and down for 5 to 10 seconds or until well mixed.

Remove the mixing glass and double strain the drink through a cocktail strainer that fits on top of the shaker into a strainer on the top of a sugar-rimmed glass; this will remove all bits of basil. Garnish with a curl of lemon zest.

SERVES A VARIABLE NUMBER

Photograph on page 36.

Watermelon Margaritas

4   cups (1-inch chunks) seedless watermelon
3/4 cup tequila
1/2 cup Triple Sec
1/3 cup sugar
1/3 cup fresh lime juice
1/4 cup fresh lemon juice
2   cups ice

Freeze the watermelon in a freezer container until firm. Combine the frozen watermelon with the tequila, Triple Sec, sugar, lime juice and lemon juice in a blender; process until smooth. Add the ice in batches, processing to the desired consistency. Pour into glasses.

SERVES 4

Lawn Boy

1   (12-ounce) can frozen limeade concentrate
12   ounces (1 1/2 cups) vodka
1/2 cup fresh mint leaves
     Ice

Combine the frozen limeade concentrate with the vodka in a blender. Add the mint leaves and fill the blender with ice. Process until slushy. Pour into glasses and serve immediately.

SERVES 4

Trapnall Hall

Located on East Capitol Avenue, Trapnall Hall has been the official receiving hall of the governor of Arkansas since the mid-1970s. With Greek Revival-style architecture, this structure was one of the first brick homes in Little Rock when it was constructed in 1843. For decades, it was the residence of many prominent Arkansans before being purchased by Mrs. Charles Minor (Julia) Taylor in 1929. She then gifted the hall to the Junior League of Little Rock. The JLLR used the building as its headquarters for more than forty years and sponsored a major restoration in the 1960s, which led to the Hall's listing on the National Register of Historic Places. In 1976, the JLLR sold this treasured site to the State of Arkansas. The Hall continues to be used frequently by the community.

Mother-in-Law Mix

2	(32-ounce) cans clamato juice	1	tablespoon prepared horseradish
	Juice of 1 lime	1/2	teaspoon salt
1/4	cup Worcestershire sauce	1/4	teaspoon pepper
1/4	cup hot sauce	16	ounces (2 cups) vodka
1	bunch fresh cilantro, chopped		

Combine the clamato juice, lime juice, Worcestershire sauce and hot sauce in a container. Add the cilantro, horseradish, salt and pepper and mix well. Chill for 8 hours or longer.

Strain into a pitcher. Combine three parts of the mix and one part vodka with ice in a glass and mix well.

SERVES 12

Red Wine Sangria

1	bottle red wine	1	cup lemon-lime soda
1	cup Triple Sec	1/4	cup each chopped apple and
1	cup apricot brandy		sliced cucumber, for garnish
2	cups orange juice		

Mix the wine, Triple Sec, brandy, orange juice and soda gently in a glass pitcher. Pour into glasses and garnish each with apple and cucumber.

SERVES 8

Pickled Okra

There is no better Arkansas garnish for a Bloody Mary than pickled okra. Wash and drain three pounds of okra. Prick the okra with a fork and pack into clean jars. Add one to two tablespoons of fresh dill or one to two teaspoons dried dill to each jar. Combine three cups of water, three cups of vinegar, and six tablespoons of salt in a saucepan. Boil until the salt is completely dissolved. Pour evenly into the jars, cap the jars, and process for five minutes in a boiling water bath.

White Sangria

$^1/_2$ cup apple liqueur
$^1/_4$ cup brandy
$^1/_2$ cup sugar
1   lime, sliced
1   lemon, sliced
1   pear, cut into wedges
1   peach, cut into wedges
2   green apples, cut into wedges
2   bottles dry white wine
2   cups club soda
1   pint fresh strawberries, cut into quarters

Combine the apple liqueur, brandy and sugar in a large pitcher and stir to dissolve the sugar completely. Add the lime, lemon, pear, peach and apples. Add the wine and mix gently. Chill for several hours. Pour into glasses and add a splash of club soda and fresh strawberries.

SERVES 10

The Little Rock Arsenal

Built in the pioneering days of Arkansas, the Little Rock Arsenal was constructed in 1840 primarily as a simple arms depot, but it gained more strategic importance during the Civil War. For a time, Confederate forces used the outpost for the manufacture of gunpowder and the repair of small arms. In 1880, General Douglas MacArthur was born on the northwest upper floor while his father, Captain Arthur MacArthur, was stationed there. Listed in the National Register of Historic Places, the Tower Building of the Arsenal is open for visitors today as the MacArthur Museum of Arkansas Military History. March on over for an overview from territorial times to the twenty-first century!

Soups &
Salads

Relish Little Rock's Accomplishments

Clinton Presidential Center

The William J. Clinton Presidential Center is the latest "star" in Little Rock's crown. Situated on the banks of the Arkansas River in a beautifully landscaped public park, the $160 million complex opened in the autumn of 2004 to international rave reviews. Here you will discover the permanent home of the largest presidential archive in American history. With interactive exhibits, complete with full-scale replicas of the Oval Office and Cabinet Room, the center attracts thousands of visitors annually from all over the world. The Clinton School of Public Service—a graduate degree program with the University of Arkansas—is located in the adjacent Sturgis Hall. One tip: come hungry and enjoy lunch in the Center's Café 42. It has a menu designed to satisfy, no matter your political taste. With President Clinton's Arkansas residence on the top floor of the library, you never know who might be lunching with you!

Italian Chili

12	ounces ground round		1	teaspoon sugar
12	ounces hot pork sausage		1	teaspoon Italian seasoning
1¹/2	cups chopped celery		1	teaspoon dried oregano
2	pounds zucchini, thinly sliced		¹/2	teaspoon dried basil
1¹/2	cups chopped bell peppers		¹/2	teaspoon garlic powder
1	cup chopped onion		2	teaspoons salt
1	(14-ounce) can red beans (optional)			Pepper to taste
1	(28-ounce) can crushed tomatoes		¹/2 to 1 cup water	
1	(28-ounce) can diced tomatoes			Grated Parmesan cheese

Brown the ground beef and sausage in a large saucepan, stirring until crumbly; drain. Add the celery and cook for 10 minutes or until the celery is tender. Add the zucchini, bell peppers, onion, beans, crushed tomatoes, diced tomatoes, sugar, Italian seasoning, oregano, basil, garlic powder, salt and pepper. Add enough water to give the desired consistency and mix well. Simmer for 40 minutes, stirring occasionally. Ladle into soup bowls and sprinkle with Parmesan cheese. Serve with crusty bread.

SERVES 8 TO 10

Opening Day

"I will always remember November 18, 2004—the day we officially opened the William J. Clinton Presidential Library and the University of Arkansas Clinton School of Public Service. After the opening, I had the privilege of escorting President and Mrs. Clinton, President and Mrs. George W. Bush, President and Mrs. George H.W. Bush, and President and Mrs. Jimmy Carter on a library tour. Growing up, I never thought I would ever meet a president—much less know one. But on that special day and for the first time in Little Rock's history, four presidents were here together."

—James L. "Skip" Rutherford III
Dean of the University of Arkansas Clinton School of Public Service

Mexican-Style Chili

Scott McGehee, *Chef/Proprietor, Boulevard Bread Company*

Mexican-Style Chili

Scott McGehee, *Chef/Proprietor, Boulevard Bread Company*

Mexican-Style Chili

Scott McGehee, *Chef/Proprietor, Boulevard Bread Company*

Mexican-Style Chili

Scott McGehee, *Chef/Proprietor, Boulevard Bread Company*

45

2 onions, chopped
6 garlic cloves, minced
2 tablespoons cumin seeds, toasted and ground
2 tablespoons vegetable oil
4 red bell peppers, chopped
4 green poblano chiles, chopped
1/4 cup chili powder
1 tablespoon ground cinnamon
1 tablespoon ground coriander
1 tablespoon pepper
1 1/2 pounds ground beef

1 pound pork shoulder or loin, cut into small cubes
2 tablespoons vegetable oil
5 cups seeded chopped tomatoes
24 ounces Mexican beer
2 or 3 canned chipotle chiles, chopped
1 teaspoon salt
1/4 cup grated unsweetened chocolate
Chopped green onions
Jack cheese, sour cream and chopped fresh cilantro, for garnish

Sauté the onions, garlic and cumin in 2 tablespoons vegetable oil in a sauté pan until the onions are translucent. Add the red bell peppers and poblano chiles and sauté over medium heat for 5 minutes. Stir in the chili powder, cinnamon, coriander and pepper. Sauté for 5 minutes longer.

Brown the ground beef and pork in 2 tablespoons vegetable oil in a large saucepan. Add the sautéed vegetables, tomatoes, beer, chipotle chiles and salt. Simmer for 1 to 1 1/2 hours. Adjust the seasoning and skim any oil from the surface.

Stir in the chocolate just before serving. Ladle into soup bowls and garnish with green onions, cheese, sour cream and cilantro.

You may add kidney beans to the chili, if desired.

SERVES 8 TO 10

"I am a strong advocate for farmers' markets and for sound and sustainable agriculture. There is nothing more joyous for me than to meet the farmers and experience the love that they put into their craft."

—Scott McGehee

Frosted Cucumber Soup

2	seedless cucumbers, chopped, or 2 cucumbers, seeded and chopped	1	teaspoon lemon juice
1	envelope cream of leek soup mix	3	drops (or less) of green food coloring
2¹/₂ cups milk		1	cup sour cream
		4 to 6 mint sprigs, for garnish	

*C*ombine the cucumbers, soup mix, milk, lemon juice, food coloring and ³/4 cup of the sour cream in a blender. Process at medium speed until smooth and evenly colored. Chill for several hours. Spoon into small soup bowls and top with the remaining sour cream. Garnish with mint sprigs.

SERVES 4 TO 6

Gazpacho Verde

3	cucumbers, peeled, seeded and coarsely chopped	1 or 2 garlic cloves, minced	
1	yellow bell pepper, coarsely chopped	2	cups chicken broth
		1¹/₂	cups plain yogurt
1	red bell pepper, coarsely chopped	1¹/₂	cups sour cream
1	avocado, coarsely chopped	2	teaspoons white wine vinegar
4	green onions, coarsely chopped		Juice of 1 lime
1	jalapeño chile, seeded and minced		Dash of hot sauce
		1¹/₂	teaspoons kosher salt
2	tablespoons finely chopped cilantro	¹/₂	teaspoon cayenne pepper
			Cilantro and chopped avocado, for garnish

*P*lace the cucumbers, yellow bell pepper, red bell pepper, one avocado, the green onions, jalapeño chile, 2 tablespoons cilantro and the garlic in a bowl. Add the chicken broth, yogurt, sour cream, vinegar, lime juice, hot sauce, kosher salt and cayenne pepper and mix well.

Process the mixture in batches in a blender until very smooth. Combine the batches in a large bowl and mix well; adjust the seasoning. Chill in the refrigerator for 2 hours or longer. Ladle into soup bowls and garnish with additional cilantro and chopped avocado.

SERVES 8

League Luncheon

Goat Cheese Mousse

23

Gazpacho Verde

46

Basil and Spinach Salad with Peppered Salmon

66

Prosciutto-Wrapped Asparagus

131

Berrytini Mousse

232

Wine: Austrian Gruner Veltliner

Gazpacho

1 cup peeled chopped tomato	2 cups tomato juice
1/2 cup each finely chopped green bell pepper, celery and cucumber	2 tablespoons balsamic vinegar
	2 tablespoons olive oil
1/4 cup finely chopped green onions	1/2 teaspoon Worcestershire sauce
2 tablespoons chopped fresh parsley	1 teaspoon salt
	1/4 teaspoon pepper
1 garlic clove, minced	1 cup plain nonfat yogurt

Combine the tomato, green bell pepper, celery, cucumber, green onions, parsley and garlic in a bowl. Add the tomato juice, vinegar, olive oil, Worcestershire sauce, salt and pepper and mix well. Process the mixture in batches in a blender until smooth. Combine the batches in a large bowl. Chill until serving time. Ladle into soup bowls and top with a dollop of yogurt.

SERVES 8

Green Chile Brie Soup

3/4 cup chopped onion	8 ounces Brie cheese, rind removed and cheese cut into small pieces
1/2 cup chopped celery	
1/4 cup (1/2 stick) butter	2 (4-ounce) cans chopped green chiles
2 tablespoons all-purpose flour	
1 (16-ounce) can chicken broth	Salt and freshly ground pepper to taste
2 cups half-and-half	

Sauté the onion and celery in the butter in a saucepan until tender. Add the flour and cook for 1 to 2 minutes, stirring constantly. Whisk in the chicken broth gradually. Add the half-and-half, cheese, green chiles, salt and pepper. Cook until the cheese melts and the soup is smooth, stirring constantly. Ladle into soup bowls.

SERVES 4 TO 6

Heifer International

Little Rock is proud to be the home of the global headquarters of one of the world's most respected humanitarian assistance partners: Heifer International. Founded in 1944, this nonprofit charitable organization is dedicated to relieving global hunger and poverty through gifts of livestock and plants, as well as education in sustainable agriculture. Through Heifer resources, more than seven million financially disadvantaged families in more than 125 countries have been significantly helped—improving their quality of life and moving them toward greater self-reliance. Heifer International headquarters is located at One World Avenue, adjacent to the Clinton Presidential Complex.

Cheese Tortellini Soup

1	large onion, chopped	1	(14-ounce) can artichoke hearts, drained and coarsely chopped
1	red bell pepper, chopped		Salt and pepper to taste
3	garlic cloves, minced	1	(9-ounce) package (or more) refrigerated cheese tortellini
2	teaspoons Italian seasoning		
	Olive oil for sautéing	6	ounces fresh spinach, chopped
6	cups chicken broth		Shredded Parmesan cheese, for garnish
1 or 2	(14-ounce) cans Great Northern beans, drained		
1	(14-ounce) can diced tomatoes		

Sauté the onion, red bell pepper and garlic with the Italian seasoning in a small amount of heated olive oil in a large heavy saucepan over medium heat. Add the chicken broth, beans, tomatoes, artichoke hearts, salt and pepper. Bring to a boil and reduce the heat. Simmer for 2 minutes.

Add the tortellini and spinach. Simmer for 5 minutes or until the tortellini is cooked through. Ladle into soup bowls and garnish with cheese.

SERVES 6

Southwestern Cheese and Corn Chowder

1	small onion, chopped	2	cups milk
2	tablespoons butter	1	cup (4 ounces) shredded Cheddar cheese
3	cups chicken broth		
2	cups fresh corn kernels	1/2	teaspoon cumin
2	potatoes, peeled and cut into 1/2-inch pieces	1/2	teaspoon salt
		1/2	teaspoon cayenne pepper
1	small red bell pepper, chopped		Crumbled crisp-cooked bacon or chopped chives, for garnish
1	rib celery, sliced		

Sauté the onion in the butter in a large saucepan for 5 minutes or until tender. Add the chicken broth, corn, potatoes, red bell pepper and celery. Bring to a boil and reduce the heat. Simmer, covered, for 5 minutes or until the potatoes are tender.

Remove 2 cups of the mixture to a blender or food processor and process until puréed. Return to the saucepan and stir in the milk, cheese, cumin, salt and cayenne pepper. Simmer for 10 minutes. Ladle into soup bowls and garnish with bacon or chives.

SERVES 6

Minestrone

1	pound bulk sweet Italian sausage, or link sausage with casings removed	1	(16-ounce) can green beans
1	cup chopped onion	1	(16-ounce) can light red or dark red kidney beans
2	ribs celery, cut into 1/4-inch slices	2	carrots, peeled and cut into 1/4-inch slices
1	garlic clove, chopped	2	cups water
1	teaspoon dried basil	4	teaspoons beef bouillon granules
1/2	teaspoon thyme	1/4	cup uncooked small elbow macaroni or shell macaroni
1/4	teaspoon pepper		
1	(15-ounce) can diced tomatoes		

Brown the sausage in a heavy saucepan sprayed with nonstick cooking spray, stirring just until the sausage is in small chunks. Remove the sausage to a bowl with a slotted spoon. Add the onion, celery and garlic to the drippings in the saucepan and sauté until tender. Stir in the basil, thyme and pepper.

Return the sausage to the saucepan and add the tomatoes, undrained green beans, undrained kidney beans, carrots, water and bouillon granules; mix well. Simmer for 30 minutes. Add the macaroni just before serving time and cook for 5 to 10 minutes or until tender. Ladle into soup bowls. Serve with a green salad and Parmesan toast. For the best flavor, prepare this a day in advance and store in the refrigerator, adding the macaroni when the soup is reheated to serve.

SERVES 6

Picadillo Cuban Stew

1	green bell pepper, chopped	1/4	cup chopped Spanish olives
2 or 3	garlic cloves, chopped	1	teaspoon ground cumin
	Olive oil for sautéing	1	teaspoon paprika
1	pound ground beef		Salt to taste
1	(15-ounce) can tomato sauce	2	teaspoons red wine vinegar
1	cup white wine	4	cups hot cooked white rice

Sauté the green bell pepper and garlic in a small amount of olive oil in a saucepan. Add the ground beef and sauté until brown and crumbly, stirring frequently; drain. Add the tomato sauce, wine, olives, cumin and paprika; mix well. Season with salt. Cook until heated through, stirring constantly. Add the vinegar and simmer for 20 minutes longer, stirring frequently. Serve over the rice.

SERVES 6 TO 8

Sherried Turkey Soup

1   onion, chopped
1/4   cup (1/2 stick) butter
3   cups sliced mushrooms
1   cup each chopped celery
     and carrots
1/4   cup all-purpose flour
6   cups low-sodium chicken broth
1   (6-ounce) package wild rice with
     seasoning, cooked

1/2   teaspoon each curry powder and
     dry mustard
1   teaspoon chervil
1   teaspoon kosher salt
1/4   teaspoon white pepper
2   cups cream
1/4   cup dry sherry
2   cups chopped cooked turkey
     or chicken

Sauté the onion in the butter in a large heavy saucepan over medium-high heat for 5 minutes or until tender. Add the mushrooms, celery and carrots and sauté for 4 minutes. Stir in the flour and cook for 1 minute.

Add the chicken broth gradually and bring to a boil, cooking until thickened and stirring constantly. Stir in the rice, curry powder, dry mustard, chervil, kosher salt and white pepper. Add the cream and sherry and simmer for 15 minutes. Add the turkey and cook until heated through. Ladle into soup bowls.

SERVES 6

Tuscan White Bean Soup

1   tablespoon olive oil
4   ounces pancetta, chopped
1   cup chopped onion
1/2   cup each chopped carrots
     and celery
2   garlic cloves, minced
4   cups chicken broth

3   (15-ounce) cans cannellini beans,
     rinsed and drained
1   each bay leaf and rosemary sprig
1/4   teaspoon kosher salt
     Freshly ground pepper to taste
1/2   cup heavy cream
     Grated Parmesan cheese to taste

Heat the olive oil in a saucepan over medium-high heat. Add the pancetta and sauté until brown and crisp. Remove with a slotted spoon. Add the onion, carrots and celery to the drippings in the saucepan and sauté for 3 minutes or until tender. Add the garlic and sauté for 2 minutes longer. Stir in the chicken broth and two cans of the beans. Add the bay leaf, rosemary, kosher salt and pepper. Bring to a simmer and simmer for 30 minutes. Remove and discard the bay leaf and rosemary.

Process the mixture with an immersion blender or in a food processor just until smooth. Add the remaining can of beans, the cream and pancetta. Cook until heated through. Ladle into soup bowls and sprinkle with cheese.

SERVES 4 TO 6

Seafood Curry Soup

3	cups finely chopped onions		2	cups light cream
1	cup finely chopped celery		5	tablespoons Madras curry powder
1	cup finely chopped tart apple		2	teaspoons salt
1/4	cup (1/2 stick) butter		1/2	teaspoon finely ground pepper
3	cups water		2	pounds shrimp, cooked, peeled
1	pound white potatoes, peeled			and cut into halves
	and chopped		1	pound lobster tails, chopped
	Salt to taste			Fresh chives, for garnish
2	cups each fish stock and			
	chicken stock			

Sauté the onions, celery and apple in the butter in a large deep skillet until the onions are golden brown. Add the water and bring to a simmer. Simmer until most of the liquid has evaporated. Purée the mixture in a blender until smooth.

Combine the potatoes with enough salted water to cover in a saucepan and bring to a boil. Cook for 5 minutes or until tender. Combine the fish stock and chicken stock in a saucepan and bring just to a simmer.

Return the purée to the skillet and whisk in the cream, curry powder, 2 teaspoons salt and the pepper. Simmer over low heat until thickened and reduced to the desired consistency. Stir in the heated stock. Add the shrimp and lobster and simmer for 10 minutes. Drain the potatoes and add to the soup. Simmer for 5 minutes longer. Ladle into soup bowls and garnish with chives.

SERVES 6 TO 8

Shellfish Bisque

1	onion, chopped		1	tablespoon crawfish boil
1	rib celery, chopped			Salt and cayenne pepper to taste
2	garlic cloves, minced		1	pound shrimp, peeled and
1/2	cup (1 stick) butter			deveined
1/2	cup all-purpose flour		8	ounces crab meat
4	cups milk			

Sauté the onion, celery and garlic in the butter in a saucepan. Add the flour gradually and cook until light brown, stirring constantly. Add the milk and crawfish boil gradually and cook until thickened, stirring constantly. Season with salt and cayenne pepper. Simmer for 45 minutes. Add the shrimp and crab meat and cook for 5 minutes or just until the shrimp are pink and cooked through. Ladle into soup bowls.

SERVES 6 TO 8

Cilantro Soup

1	bunch fresh cilantro, chopped	1/4	teaspoon salt
4	(14-ounce) cans chicken broth	1/4	teaspoon cayenne pepper
1	garlic clove, minced	1	cup sour cream
1	tablespoon butter	8	ounces cream cheese,
2	tablespoons all-purpose flour		cut into cubes
1/4	teaspoon cumin		

Process the cilantro and two cans of the chicken broth in a blender until puréed. Add the garlic and process until smooth. Melt the butter in a stockpot and stir in the flour and 1/4 cup of the remaining chicken broth. Cook until smooth, stirring constantly. Stir in the remaining chicken broth. Cook until thickened, stirring constantly. Stir in the cilantro mixture, cumin, salt and cayenne pepper. Stir in the sour cream gradually. Add the cream cheese in batches, cooking until the cream cheese melts after each addition and stirring until smooth. Ladle into soup bowls.

SERVES 4 TO 6

Butternut Squash Soup

3	cups peeled coarsely chopped	2	cups chicken broth
	butternut squash	1	cup white wine
2	carrots, cut into halves	4	cups heavy cream
1	onion, cut into wedges	1	tablespoon brown sugar (optional)
1/2	rib celery, cut into halves	1 to 2 tablespoons cinnamon	
2	garlic cloves	1 to 2 tablespoons ground cloves	
3	tablespoons butter		Salt and pepper to taste

Chop the squash, carrots, onion, celery and garlic in a food processor. Sauté the mixture in the butter in a stockpot until tender. Add the chicken broth and wine and bring to a boil. Reduce the heat and simmer for 45 minutes. Process the mixture in batches in a blender until smooth. Combine the batches in the stockpot and add the cream, brown sugar, cinnamon, cloves, salt and pepper. Cook until heated through. Ladle into soup bowls.

SERVES 6 TO 8

Pumpkin Soup Tureen

A festive and functional approach for serving soup in the fall or winter is to make a pumpkin tureen. Buy an eight- to ten-pound pumpkin and cut off the top three to four inches. Scoop out and discard the seeds. Rub the inside with cooking oil, fill with warm soup, and replace the top. Cover the pumpkin stem with foil. Place the pumpkin on a baking sheet and bake at 350 degrees for about 45 minutes or until heated through. Carefully move to a serving platter and ladle the soup into cups or bowls. The heat from the pumpkin keeps the soup warm, almost like a chafing dish.

Roasted Tomato Soup

4   pounds plum tomatoes
6   garlic cloves
3   tablespoons olive oil
1/2   teaspoon salt
1/4   teaspoon freshly cracked pepper
1   onion, finely chopped
2   teaspoons sugar
1/2   teaspoon dried oregano
2   tablespoons unsalted butter
3   cups chicken broth
1   cup heavy cream, heated
      Grated Parmesan cheese and chopped chives, for garnish

Cut the tomatoes into halves lengthwise. Place cut side up on a large baking sheet and add the garlic cloves. Drizzle with the olive oil and season with the salt and pepper. Place on the center oven rack and roast at 350 degrees for 1 hour.

Sauté the onion with the sugar and oregano in the butter in a heavy saucepan over low heat for 5 minutes or until the onion is tender. Add the tomatoes, garlic and chicken broth.

Simmer, covered, for 20 minutes. Purée in small batches in a blender. Combine the batches in the saucepan and stir in the cream. Adjust the seasoning and simmer for 2 minutes or until heated through. Ladle into soup bowls and garnish with cheese and chives. You can purée the soup with an immersion blender or strain the soup to remove the tomato skins if preferred.

SERVES 4

Apple and Cheese Salad

Apple Dressing

1/4 cup plain nonfat yogurt
1 tablespoon thawed frozen apple
   juice concentrate
1 tablespoon lime juice
1 tablespoon mayonnaise
1/4 teaspoon tarragon

Salad

1 cup chopped red apple
1 cup chopped green apple
1/2 cup chopped red grapes
1/3 cup cubed Cheddar cheese
3 tablespoons slivered
   almonds, toasted

Combine the yogurt, apple juice concentrate, lime juice, mayonnaise and tarragon in a bowl and mix well.

Toss the red apple, green apple, grapes, cheese and almonds in a bowl until combined. Add the dressing and mix gently. Chill until serving time.

Serves 6

Summer Greens and Berries

Balsamic Dijon Dressing

6 tablespoons olive oil
2 tablespoons balsamic vinegar
2 teaspoons Dijon mustard
1 tablespoon honey

Salad

8 cups mixed baby greens
1/4 cup thinly sliced red onion
1 cup fresh strawberries
1 cup fresh blueberries
1 cup fresh blackberries
1/2 cup (2 ounces) crumbled
   feta cheese
1/4 cup sliced almonds

Combine the olive oil, vinegar, Dijon mustard and honey in a bowl and mix well.

Layer the baby greens, onion, strawberries, blueberries, blackberries, cheese and almonds in a salad bowl. Drizzle with the dressing.

Serves 8

New Year's Day Gathering

Roasted Red Pepper Hummus

24

Apple and Cheese Salad

56

New Year's Peas and Sausage

97

Apple Bacon Sausage Balls

171

Chipotle Stone-Ground Corn Bread

189

Cherry Cookie Cobblers

223

Wine: Kabinett Riesling

Green Salad with Cranberry Champagne Vinaigrette

CRANBERRY CHAMPAGNE VINAIGRETTE

1   cup whole cranberry sauce
3/4 cup Champagne vinegar
1/2 cup cranberry juice
1/2 teaspoon freshly ground pepper
1/2 cup extra-virgin olive oil

SPICED PECANS

2   cups pecans
3   tablespoons melted butter

1/2 teaspoon paprika
1/2 teaspoon garlic powder
1/2 teaspoon onion powder
1/2 teaspoon salt

SALAD

Fresh salad greens
1   (11-ounce) can mandarin oranges, drained
1/2 small red onion, thinly sliced
1/4 cup chopped fresh leaf parsley

Combine the cranberry sauce, vinegar, cranberry juice and pepper in a jar with a tight-fitting lid and seal tightly. Shake well. Add the olive oil and shake to mix well.

Toss the pecans, melted butter, paprika, garlic powder, onion powder and salt in a small bowl until coated. Spread in a single layer on a baking sheet. Toast at 350 degrees for 15 minutes or until light brown.

Mix the salad greens, oranges, onion and parsley in a bowl. Sprinkle with the pecans and drizzle with the desired amount of vinaigrette.

SERVES 4 TO 6

The Clintons in Arkansas

"No matter how far we travel or what cities we visit, Little Rock will always hold a special place in our hearts. From the birth of our daughter and the joy of our life, Chelsea, to several election night victories at the Old State Capitol and years in the Governor's Mansion, we have celebrated many of our happiest moments together along the banks of the Arkansas River. Today we are proud that the Clinton Presidential Center and the Clinton School of Public Service at the University of Arkansas have been welcomed as integral parts of the Little Rock community. We look forward to every opportunity we have to return, to visit with friends and, of course, to enjoy the fine cuisine. Whether we're dining at Doe's, at a quaint restaurant in the River Market, or at any of the many other wonderful establishments in Little Rock, we always leave with our plates cleared and our stomachs full."

—President Bill Clinton and U.S. Senator Hillary Clinton

Grapefruit Avocado Salad

Scott McGehee, *Chef/Proprietor of Boulevard Bread Company*

1/2	red onion, thinly sliced			Salt and pepper to taste
2	tablespoons red wine vinegar		8	cups salad greens
1/2	cup olive oil		2	avocados, sliced
	Grated zest of 1 orange		2	sweet grapefruit, sectioned

Mix the onion with the vinegar in a small bowl and let stand for 10 to 14 minutes. Stir in the olive oil and orange zest. Season with salt and pepper.

Place the salad greens on salad plates. Arrange the avocado slices and grapefruit sections over the greens. Season the avocado with salt. Drizzle with the onion vinaigrette.

SERVES 4 TO 6

Autumn Salad

MAPLE VINAIGRETTE		SALAD	
1/2	cup walnut oil or vegetable oil	1	head red leaf lettuce, torn
1/4	cup cider vinegar	1	head Bibb lettuce, torn
2	tablespoons minced shallots	1	cup watercress leaves
2	tablespoons fresh lemon juice	1	apple, thinly sliced
1 1/2	tablespoons maple syrup	3/4	cup glazed pecans
1/4	teaspoon salt	3/4	cup (3 ounces) crumbled
1/4	teaspoon freshly ground pepper		blue cheese

Combine the walnut oil, vinegar, shallots, lemon juice, maple syrup, salt and pepper in a jar with a tight-fitting lid and seal tightly. Shake to mix well.

Toss the leaf lettuce, Bibb lettuce and watercress in a salad bowl. Arrange the apple slices over the greens and sprinkle with the pecans and cheese. Drizzle with the vinaigrette and toss gently to mix well.

SERVES 6

Arugula and Pomegranate Salad

Shallot Vinaigrette

1	chicken bouillon cube
3	tablespoons water
1	large shallot, coarsely chopped
1/3	cup white wine vinegar
1 1/2	tablespoons Dijon mustard
1	egg
1/3	cup olive oil
1/3	cup canola oil
	Salt and white pepper to taste

Salad

1	cup pecans
3/4	cup sugar
10	ounces arugula
2	apples, chopped
1	pear, chopped
	Pomegranate seeds or dried cranberries to taste
	Crumbled feta cheese to taste

Combine the bouillon cube and water in a microwave-safe bowl and microwave on High for 30 seconds; stir to dissolve the bouillon cube. Combine the shallot, vinegar, Dijon mustard and egg in a blender and process until smooth. Add the bouillon, processing constantly. Add the olive oil and canola oil gradually, processing constantly. Season with salt and white pepper.

Toast the pecans with the sugar in a heavy nonstick skillet over medium heat until the sugar melts and the pecans are coated and brown. Spread the pecans on a parchment-lined cooking sheet and allow to cool.

Combine the arugula, apples, pear and pomegranate seeds in a bowl. Add the pecans and vinaigrette and toss to mix well. Sprinkle with cheese.

If you are concerned about using uncooked eggs, use eggs pasteurized in their shells, which are sold at some specialty food stores, or use an equivalent amount of pasteurized egg substitute.

Serves 6 to 8

Orange and Hearts of Palm Salad

ORANGE VINAIGRETTE
1/4   cup mayonnaise
3   tablespoons thawed frozen orange juice concentrate
3   tablespoons white wine vinegar
1   tablespoon vegetable oil
1   teaspoon sugar

SALAD
   Bibb lettuce leaves
1   (14-ounce) can hearts of palm, drained and
   cut into thin slices
1   (11-ounce) can mandarin oranges
2   avocados
2   green onions with tender tops, thinly sliced
3   tablespoons finely chopped oil-cured black olives
1/4   cup toasted coarsely chopped pecans

Combine the mayonnaise, orange juice concentrate, vinegar, oil and sugar in a small bowl and whisk until smooth. Cover tightly and chill in the refrigerator for 24 hours.

Line the salad plates with lettuce leaves. Arrange the hearts of palm and orange sections over the lettuce. Cut the avocados into halves. Remove the seeds and scoop out balls with a melon baller. Add to the salad. Drizzle with half the vinaigrette. Sprinkle with the green onions, black olives and pecans. Serve with the remaining vinaigrette.

SERVES 6

Tomato Feta Salad

*Cut two pints of grape tomatoes into halves and place in a large bowl.
Add three-fourths cup of chopped red onion, two tablespoons of
white wine vinegar, three tablespoons of olive oil, one-half teaspoon each of salt and
pepper, and two tablespoons each of freshly chopped basil and parsley.
Toss well and fold in twelve ounces of cubed feta cheese. Serve at room temperature.
This makes a fresh and flavorful addition to any summer meal.*

Cheese Tortellini Salad

SUN-DRIED TOMATO VINAIGRETTE

1/4   cup drained oil-packed sun-dried tomatoes
4   teaspoons balsamic vinegar
4   teaspoons red wine vinegar
1   garlic clove, minced
1/3   cup extra-virgin olive oil
      Kosher salt and freshly ground pepper to taste

SALAD

1   (9-ounce) package three-cheese tortellini
1   tablespoon olive oil
1   (10-ounce) package mixed greens
1/4   cup thinly sliced drained oil-packed
      sun-dried tomatoes
5   fresh basil leaves, thinly sliced, for garnish

Process the sun-dried tomatoes, balsamic vinegar, wine vinegar and garlic in a food processor until smooth. Add the olive oil gradually, processing constantly until emulsified. Season with kosher salt and pepper.

Cook the tortellini using the package directions; rinse under cold water until cool and drain. Drizzle with the olive oil in a bowl to prevent sticking. Add the mixed greens, sun-dried tomatoes and vinaigrette; toss to coat well. Garnish with the basil.

SERVES 6

Cheese Tortellini Salad Variations

The possibilities are endless with this salad just by adding readily available ingredients from the pantry. Try including grilled chicken, black olives, chopped red onion, drained and rinsed white beans, or any other of your favorites to make this versatile dish even better!

Pear and Gorgonzola Salad Pizza

1   (12-inch) commercial pizza crust
     (tested with Boboli crust)
1   teaspoon olive oil
2   Bosc pears, thinly sliced
1   cup (4 ounces) crumbled Gorgonzola cheese
1/4 cup walnut halves, toasted
1 1/2 to 2 cups (6 to 8 ounces) shredded mozzarella cheese
4   cups mixed spring salad greens
1/2 cup (2 ounces) crumbled Gorgonzola cheese
1/4 cup Champagne vinaigrette

Brush the pizza crust with the olive oil. Arrange the pear slices in a single layer over the crust. Sprinkle with 1 cup Gorgonzola cheese and the walnuts. Top with the mozzarella cheese. Bake at 350 degrees for 10 to 12 minutes or until the cheeses are melted.

Combine the salad greens, 1/2 cup Gorgonzola cheese and the vinaigrette in a bowl and toss to mix well. Sprinkle over the pizza. Cut into wedges to serve.

SERVES 8

Warm Steak and Potato Salad

1	pound small red potatoes
3	slices bacon
1	small red onion, chopped
16	ounces boneless sirloin steak, thinly sliced
1/4	teaspoon salt
1/2	teaspoon cornstarch
1/2	teaspoon water
5	tablespoons honey
5	tablespoons cider vinegar
1	package baby spinach
1	cup grape tomatoes, cut into halves

Combine the potatoes with enough water to cover in a medium saucepan. Bring to a boil and reduce the heat. Simmer for 15 minutes or until tender.

Cook the bacon in a skillet until crisp; drain on a paper towel and crumble. Add the onion to the drippings in the skillet and sauté for 3 minutes. Add the steak and salt and sauté for 3 minutes longer. Remove to a bowl and cover to keep warm.

Blend the cornstarch and water in a cup. Add the honey and vinegar to the skillet and cook for 2 minutes. Stir the cornstarch mixture and add to the skillet. Cook for 30 seconds. Remove from the heat.

Drain the potatoes and rinse with cold water; cut into quarters. Add the potatoes, bacon, spinach, tomatoes and warm dressing to the steak; toss gently to coat well.

SERVES 6 TO 8

Baja Chicken Salad

5   chicken breasts, grilled and chopped
1   red bell pepper, chopped
1   cup frozen green peas
1   (14-ounce) can corn kernels, drained
1   (14-ounce) can black beans, rinsed and drained
1/2   cup sliced black olives
1/2   bunch green onions, chopped
1/2   cup chopped cilantro
1   cup (4 ounces) shredded pepper Jack cheese
1/4   cup mayonnaise
1/3   cup olive oil
     Juice of 1 lime
     Kosher salt and freshly ground pepper to taste
8   slices bacon, crisp-cooked and crumbled
1/4   cup sunflower seeds
     Sliced avocado, for garnish

Combine the chicken, red bell pepper, green peas, corn, black beans, black olives, green onions, cilantro and pepper Jack cheese in a large bowl. Add the mayonnaise, olive oil, lime juice, kosher salt and pepper and mix gently. Add the bacon and sunflower seeds just before serving. Garnish with sliced avocado.

SERVES 10 TO 12

Tarragon Chicken Salad

3 cups shredded cooked chicken (about 1 1/2 pounds)	1/4 cup coarse-grained mustard
1 cup quartered red grapes	2 teaspoons chopped fresh tarragon
2 ribs celery, finely chopped	1 teaspoon kosher salt or sea salt
1/2 cup chopped pecans	1 teaspoon ground red pepper
3/4 cup mayonnaise	1/2 teaspoon black pepper
	Lettuce leaves

Combine the chicken with the grapes, celery and pecans in a bowl. Add the mayonnaise, mustard, tarragon, kosher salt, red pepper and black pepper and mix well. Chill for 1 to 24 hours. Serve on lettuce leaves.

SERVES 8

Basil and Spinach Salad with Peppered Salmon

1 tablespoon olive oil	Salt and pepper to taste
1 tablespoon soy sauce	1/4 cup olive oil
1 teaspoon lemon juice	2 garlic cloves, minced
2 salmon fillets	1/4 cup pine nuts, toasted
Coarsely ground pepper	2 ounces prosciutto, chopped
3 cups spinach	1/3 cup grated Parmesan cheese
1 cup fresh basil	

Mix the olive oil, soy sauce and lemon juice in a shallow dish. Add the salmon and marinate for 15 minutes, turning once.

Pat the salmon dry and coat generously with coarsely ground pepper. Grill the salmon for 4 minutes on each side or until done to taste.

Combine the spinach and basil in a large salad bowl and season with salt and pepper. Heat the olive oil in a sauté pan. Add the garlic, pine nuts and prosciutto. Sauté for 3 to 4 minutes. Combine the sautéed mixture with the spinach and basil. Add the cheese and toss to mix well. Spoon the mixture onto salad plates and top with the salmon.

SERVES 2

Coastal Shrimp Salad

HONEY MUSTARD DRESSING

1/4 cup Dijon mustard
3 tablespoons honey
1/4 cup cider vinegar
1/2 teaspoon sea salt
3/4 cup olive oil

SALAD

10 ounces romaine lettuce
3/4 cup chopped cilantro
1 cucumber, peeled, sliced and cut into quarters
1 red bell pepper, chopped
2 cups pineapple chunks
1 (8-ounce) can sliced water chestnuts, drained
1 cup cashew halves and pieces
16 to 18 large fresh Carolina or Gulf Coast shrimp, peeled and deveined
3 to 4 tablespoons olive oil
3 to 4 tablespoons butter
Juice of 2 limes

Combine the Dijon mustard, honey, vinegar and sea salt in a bowl and mix well. Add the olive oil in a fine stream, whisking constantly. Chill until serving time.

Toss the lettuce with the cilantro in a bowl. Chill in the refrigerator. Arrange the lettuce mixture on salad plates. Sprinkle the cucumber, red bell pepper, pineapple, water chestnuts and cashews evenly over the lettuce.

Sauté the shrimp in the olive oil and butter in a 10-inch sauté pan for 4 minutes or until pink and opaque. Arrange the shrimp over the salads and drizzle with the lime juice and the desired amount of the dressing.

SERVES 4

Little Rock Healthcare Systems

The University of Arkansas for Medical Sciences serves as the foundation for Arkansas healthcare. The state-of-the-art University Hospital and outpatient clinics of the University of Arkansas for Medical Sciences, along with its affiliates, Arkansas Children's Hospital and the Central Arkansas Veterans Hospital, are world leaders in many areas of care. Known to all who walk through its doors as "a place of care, love, and hope," Arkansas Children's Hospital is one of the nation's largest centers for pediatric care. Baptist Health, the state's largest not-for-profit healthcare network, and St. Vincent Infirmary Medical Center both call Little Rock home, offering major-league healing hands around the clock.

Cilantro Lime Shrimp on Mesclun Greens

Jason Knapp, *Executive Chef of The Governor's Mansion*

CILANTRO LIME VINAIGRETTE

- 1/4 cup lime juice
- 2 tablespoons chopped cilantro
- 1 tablespoon Dijon mustard
- 1 tablespoon honey
- 1 teaspoon Tabasco sauce
  Salt to taste
- 1/2 cup canola oil

SALAD

- 10 (12-count) shrimp, cleaned and deveined
- 1 package mixed spring salad greens
- 1 red bell pepper, chopped into 1/4-inch pieces
- 2 ribs celery, sliced
- 1 avocado, sliced

Combine the lime juice, cilantro, Dijon mustard, honey, Tabasco sauce and salt in a food processor and pulse 3 to 5 times to mix well. Add the canola oil gradually, processing constantly until emulsified. Divide the mixture into two portions. Reserve one portion in the refrigerator for the dressing.

Add the shrimp to the remaining vinaigrette. Marinate in the refrigerator for 2 to 4 hours. Drain, discarding the marinade. Grill the shrimp for 2 minutes on each side or just until cooked through.

Toss the salad greens with 2 tablespoons of the reserved vinaigrette. Arrange on the salad plates. Sprinkle with the red bell pepper and celery. Arrange the avocado slices over the top and the shrimp around the edge. Serve with the remaining vinaigrette, if desired.

SERVES 2

Lion's World Services for the Blind

Founded in 1947 by the late Roy Kumpe, Lion's World Services for the Blind was created to serve those who are blind and visually impaired. From its headquarters facilities in Little Rock, this landmark institution has been recognized as one of the most respected and comprehensive rehabilitation centers in the world. Training programs and a variety of other vocational/psychological resources have aided hundreds from throughout the globe in functioning independently and productively in "sighted society." Thanks to the confidence and will to succeed developed by this center, a new day is continually dawning for those who profit from this life-changing experience.

Decadent Blue Cheese Wedge Salad

BLUE CHEESE DRESSING
1   cup mayonnaise
1   cup sour cream
1/2 cup buttermilk
2   tablespoons grated onion
4   dashes of hot sauce
1   tablespoon lemon juice
1 1/2 teaspoons Worcestershire sauce
1   teaspoon minced garlic
1   teaspoon sugar
1 1/2 cups (6 ounces) crumbled
     blue cheese

1   teaspoon white pepper
1/2 teaspoon cayenne pepper

SALAD
1   head iceberg lettuce, cut into
     8 wedges
8   slices bacon, crisp-cooked
     and crumbled
     Salt and pepper to taste
     Chopped green onions and
     crumbled blue cheese, for garnish

Combine the mayonnaise, sour cream and buttermilk in a bowl and mix well. Add the onion, hot sauce, lemon juice, Worcestershire sauce, garlic, sugar, cheese, white pepper and cayenne pepper and mix well. Chill for 24 hours.

Place the lettuce wedges on salad plates. Spoon the dressing over the wedges and sprinkle with the bacon; season with salt and pepper. Garnish with green onions and additional blue cheese.

SERVES 8

Fatoush Salad

1   cup red bell pepper strips
1   cup green bell pepper strips
1   cup peeled thinly sliced cucumber
1/2 cup thinly sliced onion
2   tablespoons chopped fresh mint
2   tablespoons chopped
     fresh cilantro

2   tablespoons fresh lemon juice
2   teaspoons extra-virgin olive oil
1/2 teaspoon salt
1/4 teaspoon pepper
2   tomatoes, cut into 1/4-inch wedges
1   (6-inch) pita round, toasted and
     torn into bite-size pieces

Combine the red bell pepper, green bell pepper, cucumber, onion, mint and cilantro in a bowl. Add the lemon juice, olive oil, salt and pepper and toss to coat well. Arrange the tomato wedges and pita pieces over the salad.

SERVES 4

Fiesta Salad

1	(14-ounce) can diced tomatoes, drained	1	tablespoon chopped fresh basil
2	cups fresh or frozen corn kernels	1	teaspoon chopped garlic
1	red bell pepper, chopped	1/4	cup olive oil or canola oil
1	cup chopped red onion	1	tablespoon cumin
1/2	cup chopped celery	1 1/2	teaspoons garlic powder
1	(2-ounce) can sliced black olives, drained	1 1/2	teaspoons chili powder
1	(14-ounce) can artichoke hearts, sliced	1/2	teaspoon oregano
			Salt to taste
1	(14-ounce) can black-eyed peas, drained	1/2	teaspoon pepper

Combine the tomatoes, corn, red bell pepper, onion, celery, black olives, undrained artichoke hearts, peas, basil and garlic in a bowl and mix well. Add the olive oil, cumin, garlic powder, chili powder, oregano, salt and pepper and mix to coat evenly. You can vary the type and amount of seasonings used to suit your taste.

SERVES 10 TO 12

Tangy Poppy Seed Dressing

Combine six tablespoons of olive oil, one tablespoon of honey, two tablespoons of red wine vinegar, one teaspoon of honey Dijon mustard, one-half teaspoon of poppy seeds, one-half teaspoon of salt, and a pinch of cayenne pepper in a jar with a lid and seal tightly. Shake well before serving.

Soaked Salad Dressing

Combine the juice of two lemons with one tablespoon of olive oil, two tablespoons of white wine vinegar, two garlic cloves, and one tablespoon of Worcestershire sauce in a small bowl. Add salt and freshly ground pepper to taste. Drizzle over fresh salad greens and let soak for several minutes before serving. This goes very well with salads with olives and cheese.

Fumi Salad

1/4 cup sugar
2 teaspoons salt
1 teaspoon pepper
6 tablespoons vinegar
1 cup olive oil
1/2 cup slivered almonds

1/2 cup sesame seeds
1 tablespoon margarine
1 head cabbage, finely chopped
8 green onions, finely chopped
Noodles from 2 packages ramen
noodles, crushed

Mix the sugar with the salt and pepper in a small saucepan. Add the vinegar and olive oil and mix well. Heat just until the sugar and seasonings dissolve, stirring constantly; do not boil.

Sauté the almonds and sesame seeds in the margarine in a skillet over low heat until light brown. Combine with the cabbage, green onions and crushed noodles in a large salad bowl.

Pour the dressing over the cabbage mixture and toss to mix well. Chill in the refrigerator for several hours before serving.

SERVES 8

Girls' Night In Salad

BALSAMIC VINAIGRETTE
1/3 cup olive oil
1/4 cup white balsamic vinegar
Salt and pepper to taste

SALAD
1 head red leaf lettuce
1 package mixed spring salad
greens

1/2 to 1 red onion, sliced
1 cup grape tomatoes
1 small container blueberries
1 small apple, chopped
1 avocado, chopped
1 (15-ounce) can garbanzo
beans, drained
1/2 cup pecan halves
Crumbled feta cheese to taste

Combine the olive oil, vinegar, salt and pepper in a jar with a lid and seal tightly. Shake to mix well.

Toss the lettuce and salad greens with the onion, tomatoes, blueberries, apple, avocado, beans, pecans and cheese in a large bowl. Shake the vinaigrette and add to the salad at serving time; toss gently to mix well.

SERVES 6 TO 8

Warm Cheese and Romaine Salad

DIJON VINAIGRETTE

2	tablespoons red wine vinegar
1	tablespoon Dijon mustard
1/2	cup olive oil
2	tablespoons finely chopped shallots
	Salt and pepper to taste

SALAD

1/2	cup bread crumbs
1 1/2	tablespoons grated Parmesan cheese
1 1/2	tablespoons sesame seeds
3	(4-ounce) rolls herbed goat cheese
1	egg, beaten
6	cups torn romaine lettuce
24	kalamata olives
24	grape tomatoes
3	tablespoons butter

Combine the vinegar and Dijon mustard in a bowl and mix well. Add the olive oil in a fine stream, whisking constantly. Whisk in the shallots, salt and pepper.

Mix the bread crumbs, Parmesan cheese and sesame seeds in a bowl. Cut each goat cheese roll into eight slices. Dip the slices into the egg and coat with the bread crumb mixture. Chill, covered, for 30 minutes or longer.

Toss the romaine lettuce with the dressing and spoon onto salad plates. Add the olives and grape tomatoes to the plates.

Melt the butter in a skillet over medium heat. Add the goat cheese medallions and sauté for 1 to 2 minutes on each side or until brown. Drain on paper towels. Arrange in the centers of the salads and serve while the cheese is still warm.

SERVES 6

The Little Rock Marathon

Since 2003, the Little Rock Marathon has been applauded throughout the nation as one of the premier running events of the spring season. The certified 26.2-mile single-loop course begins and ends downtown after taking participants past historic sites, through scenic neighborhoods, and then along the Arkansas River trail. A variety of race options are offered with varying individual and relay lengths as a means to raise funds for Little Rock Parks and Recreation. The USATF-sanctioned competition is a qualifying event for the Boston Marathon and is the first race in the state to be transponder-chip timed. Chalk up this annual highlight as yet another way we are setting the pace in Little Rock!

German Potato Salad

6	slices bacon, chopped		$1/8$	teaspoon pepper
2	teaspoons all-purpose flour		3	cups chopped boiled potatoes
2	tablespoons water		$1/2$	cup chopped green onions
$1/4$	cup vinegar			Chopped parsley to taste
3	tablespoons sugar			

Fry the bacon in a skillet until crisp; drain on paper towels. Stir the flour into the drippings in the skillet and cook until smooth. Add the water, vinegar, sugar and pepper and mix well. Cook until thickened, stirring constantly.

Pour the mixture over the potatoes in a bowl and keep warm until serving time. Add the bacon, green onions and parsley and mix gently. Serve immediately.

SERVES 4

Roasted Red Pepper Salad

BALSAMIC DRESSING

$1/3$	cup balsamic vinegar
1	teaspoon sugar
$1/2$	teaspoon salt
$1/2$	teaspoon pepper
$2/3$	cup extra-virgin olive oil

SALAD

1	package mixed salad greens
1	cup (4 ounces) crumbled goat cheese
1	large red bell pepper

Combine the vinegar, sugar, salt and pepper in a blender and process until smooth. Add the olive oil in a thin stream, processing constantly until emulsified. Serve immediately or let stand at room temperature for up to 10 hours.

Place the salad greens in a salad bowl and top with the goat cheese. Cut the red bell pepper into halves lengthwise. Place cut side down on a lightly greased baking sheet. Broil until the skin is blistered and blackened. Place in a plastic bag and let stand for 3 to 5 minutes. Peel away the skin and cut the pepper into strips.

Add the hot bell pepper strips to the salad greens and cheese and toss to mix well and melt the cheese. Add the dressing and toss again. Serve immediately.

SERVES 6

Meats &
Main Dishes

Junior League of Little Rock
Serving Others

Junior League of Little Rock

Originally built in 1910, the Woman's City Club building is currently the headquarters of the Junior League of Little Rock. The three-story brick structure is located at 401 South Scott in downtown Little Rock and has been on the National Register of Historic Places for more than twenty-five years. Ironically, this landmark was used as a men's social club until 1927 and then for the next seventy-four years was a clubhouse for women's social and community clubs. The League purchased the building in 2001 and after a seven-figure renovation occupied the facility for its headquarters in 2002. Renamed the Junior League of Little Rock in 2006, this historic site is utilized by the membership and the community as a site for meetings and events. For the JLLR, it's "action central" and offers others a taste of the League's home.

Balsamic Beef Tenderloin

2 shallots, chopped	¹/2 cup extra-virgin olive oil
3 or 4 garlic cloves, minced	¹/2 teaspoon salt
2 tablespoons extra-virgin olive oil	¹/2 teaspoon freshly ground pepper
¹/2 cup balsamic vinegar	1 (4-pound) beef tenderloin,
¹/4 cup sugar	trimmed

Sauté the shallots and garlic in 2 tablespoons olive oil in a sauté pan until the scallions are translucent. Combine with the vinegar, sugar, ¹/2 cup olive oil, the salt and pepper in a sealable plastic bag. Add the tenderloin and seal; turn to coat well. Marinate in the refrigerator for 24 hours, turning several times.

Drain the tenderloin, reserving the marinade. Grill for 12 minutes, turning every 3 minutes to mark all four sides. Remove to a baking dish and add the reserved marinade. Roast at 375 degrees for about 7 minutes per pound for medium-rare, 145 degrees on a meat thermometer, or to 160 degrees for medium; the temperature will continue to rise 5 to 10 degrees after the tenderloin is removed from the oven. Let stand at room temperature for 15 minutes. Slice to serve.

SERVES 8

Blue Cheese-Stuffed Tenderloin

1 (3- to 4-pound) whole	1 bunch chives, chopped
beef tenderloin	2 cups (8 ounces) crumbled
1 cup Italian bread crumbs	blue cheese
1 garlic clove, crushed	Olive oil

Ask the butcher to trim out the tenderloin. Butterfly the tenderloin by slicing it lengthwise, cutting to but not through one side. Open up the tenderloin and sprinkle the cut sides with the bread crumbs, garlic and chives. Add as much of the blue cheese as possible to allow the sides to close well and keep the cheese from running out during the roasting period.

Close the sides and secure in several places with kitchen twine. Rub with olive oil. Place on a rack in a roasting pan. Place in an oven preheated to 500 degrees and reduce the temperature to 425 degrees. Roast for 30 to 45 minutes or until done to taste. Remove the twine. Cut the tenderloin into 1-inch slices to serve.

SERVES 6 TO 8

Peppercorn Beef Tenderloin

2   (3-pound) beef tenderloins
3   tablespoons Dijon mustard
2   tablespoons olive oil
3   garlic cloves, chopped
1   tablespoon dried sage
1/4 cup mixed green, red and black
     peppercorns, cracked

Cut lengthwise pockets in the tenderloins, leaving 1 inch uncut at both ends. Combine the Dijon mustard, olive oil, garlic and sage in a bowl and mix well. Spread in the pockets and over the outside of the tenderloins. Place one-third of the cracked peppercorns in the pockets and secure in three places with kitchen twine.

Press the remaining peppercorns over the outside of the tenderloins. Place seam side down on a rack in a roasting pan. Roast at 425 degrees for 30 to 45 minutes or to 145 degrees on a meat thermometer for medium-rare or to 160 degrees for medium. Let stand at room temperature for 10 minutes. Remove the twine. Cut the tenderloins into slices to serve.

SERVES 10

Special Steak Sauce

Combine three tablespoons of ketchup, one tablespoon of Worcestershire sauce, three tablespoons of butter, three tablespoons of vinegar, one teaspoon of prepared mustard, and salt and pepper to taste in a small saucepan. Simmer for 15 minutes. Serve hot or store in the refrigerator. Enjoy on your favorite meat.

Beef Brisket

1	(10-ounce) can beef consommé	1	tablespoon liquid smoke
1/2	cup plus 2 tablespoons soy sauce		Garlic powder to taste
1/4	cup lemon juice	1	(4-pound) beef brisket

Combine the beef consommé, lemon juice, liquid smoke and garlic powder in a bowl and mix well. Pour over the brisket in a roasting pan. Marinate, covered, in the refrigerator for 12 hours, basting once or twice. Roast, covered, at 300 degrees for 4 hours.

SERVES 8

Gorgonzola Fillets with Balsamic Fig Reduction

4	(8-ounce) beef fillets	3	tablespoons fig preserves
	Salt and freshly ground pepper	1/2	cup (2 ounces) crumbled
	to taste		Gorgonzola cheese
1 1/2	cups balsamic vinegar		

Season the fillets with salt and pepper. Combine the vinegar and preserves in a small saucepan and cook over medium-high heat for 15 minutes or until thickened and reduced by one-half.

Heat a broiler pan in a preheated broiler and place the fillets in the pan. Broil for 7 minutes on each side for medium-rare, 135 degrees on a meat thermometer. Sprinkle with the cheese and broil for 1 minute longer or until the cheese melts and begins to brown.

Let stand at room temperature for several minutes. Drizzle each fillet with 1 tablespoon of the balsamic fig reduction and pour the remaining reduction into a bowl to serve with the fillets.

The reduction is also good on vegetables, such as asparagus or green beans.

SERVES 4

Riverfest

Memorial Day weekend brings Riverfest to Little Rock. Grab your family and come down to the Riverfront Park for Arkansas's largest and most popular music, art, and food festival. The fun began in 1977 when the Junior League of Little Rock brought the American Wind Symphony to the city for an event called the Summer Arts Festival. The success of this event evolved into Riverfest. Today about a quarter of a million festival-goers enjoy its offerings. At a given moment, four musical acts might be playing across the banks of the Arkansas River. If food is the key, be prepared for a virtual smorgasbord of choices to satisfy every taste for every age. It will make your Memorial Day weekend even more memorable!

Roast Beef with Burgundy Mushroom Gravy

1   (4-pound) boneless chuck roast
    Salt and freshly ground pepper to taste
2   tablespoons olive oil
2   tablespoons butter
2   onions, sliced
16 ounces mushrooms, stems removed and
    mushrooms sliced
3   large garlic cloves, chopped
1   cup burgundy or other dry red wine
1/2 cup Cognac or good-quality bourbon
2   cups beef broth
1   tablespoon tomato paste
1   sprig of fresh thyme
1   sprig of fresh rosemary
1   tablespoon butter
2   tablespoons all-purpose flour
    Toasted crusty country bread

Pat the roast dry with paper towels and season with salt and pepper. Heat the olive oil in a large Dutch oven over medium-high heat. Add the roast and brown on all sides. Remove the roast to a plate.

Add 2 tablespoons butter and the onions to the drippings in the Dutch oven and sauté for 5 minutes or until the onions are tender. Add the mushrooms and garlic and sauté for 2 minutes longer.

Stir in the wine and Cognac and bring to a boil. Cook for 1 minute and stir in the beef broth and tomato paste. Return the roast to the Dutch oven and add the thyme and rosemary. Bring to a boil and cover.

Place in the oven and roast at 350 degrees for 3 hours or until the roast is fork-tender, turning it after 1 1/2 hours. Remove to a cutting board. Discard the thyme and rosemary.

Place the vegetables and cooking liquid in a food processor and process until smooth. Return the mixture to the Dutch oven. Blend 1 tablespoon butter with the flour in a cup with a fork. Add to the Dutch oven and simmer until thickened, stirring constantly.

Slice the roast and serve on the bread. Spoon the gravy over the top.

SERVES 6

Nutcracker Dinner

Poinsettia Cocktail

37

Spicy Brie Tarts

27

Prime Rib with Horseradish Sauce

81

Broccoli with Lemon Crumbs

135

Caramelized Onion and White Cheddar Potatoes

144

Apple Raisin Compote

229

Molten Chocolate Cakes with Orange Cranberry Cream

203

Wine: California Chardonnay

Prime Rib with Horseradish Sauce

HORSERADISH SAUCE

1/3 cup ground horseradish
2/3 cup mayonnaise (tested with Hellman's)
     Juice of 1/2 lemon

PRIME RIB

1   (3- to 6-pound) prime rib roast or choice rib roast
     Olive oil
     Worcestershire sauce
     Grill and steak seasoning
     Kosher salt

Combine the horseradish, mayonnaise and lemon juice in a bowl and mix well. Store in the refrigerator. Bring to room temperature to serve.

Ask the butcher to bone the prime rib and secure with twine. Let stand at room temperature for 2 hours before roasting. Rub the roast with olive oil and Worcestershire sauce. Press grill and steak seasoning and kosher salt over all surfaces, covering completely. Let stand at room temperature for 1 hour.

Place the roast on its side on a rack in a broiler pan and add water to the broiler pan. Broil for 5 to 6 minutes on each side to sear. Turn the oven temperature to 300 degrees. Place the roast on end and insert a meat thermometer into the thickest portion. Roast for 12 to 13 minutes per pound, 130 degrees for rare or 140 degrees for medium-rare. Remove the twine. Slice the prime rib and serve.

SERVES 6 TO 12

French Dips

French Dip Sandwiches are a great way to feed any hungry crowd. To prepare, place a three- to five-pound rump roast in a large stockpot and add ten beef bouillon cubes, one teaspoon of oregano, three bay leaves, three crushed garlic cloves, two tablespoons of sugar, and two large sliced onions. Pour in one can of beer and three beer cans of water. Cover and simmer for at least three hours or until the roast is tender. Remove the roast to a cutting board, reserving the pan juices. Thinly slice the roast and serve with the onions in a split baguette. Strain the reserved pan juices. Serve the reserved pan juices or au jus in individual side dishes for dipping. This dish can also be prepared in a slow cooker.

Rib-Eye Steaks with Cowboy Butter

COWBOY BUTTER
1   cup (2 sticks) unsalted
     butter, softened
1/4 cup chopped cilantro leaves
3   garlic cloves, minced
1   tablespoon kosher salt

STEAKS
4   rib-eye steaks
     Salt and pepper to taste
     Olive oil

Combine the butter, cilantro, garlic and kosher salt in a food processor and process until smooth. Shape into a roll 1 1/2 inches in diameter on waxed paper, removing any air pockets. Wrap tightly and secure with tape. Place in the freezer for 1 hour before serving or store in the freezer for up to 1 month.

Sprinkle the steaks with salt and pepper; drizzle with olive oil. Let stand for 1 hour to come to room temperature. Grill over medium-high heat until done to taste. Slice the butter and serve on the steaks.

SERVES 4

Flank Steak Tournedos

1   (1 1/2-pound) flank steak
     Meat tenderizer to taste
1   teaspoon garlic salt
1/2 teaspoon coarsely ground pepper

6 to 8 slices bacon, partially cooked
       but not crisp
8   ounces mushrooms, finely chopped
1/2 bunch parsley, chopped

Ask the butcher to run the steak through the tenderizer twice. Place the steak on a work surface and sprinkle lightly with meat tenderizer. Sprinkle with the garlic salt and pepper. Arrange the bacon lengthwise on the steak, covering as much of the steak as possible. Top with the mushrooms and parsley.

Roll the steak from the narrow end to enclose the filling and secure with wooden picks. Cut into 1-inch tournedos, securing with additional wooden picks if necessary. Grill over medium heat for 5 to 7 minutes on each side. Remove the wooden picks before serving. You can prepare the tournedos ahead and chill for up to 24 hours before grilling.

SERVES 4

The Greatest Hamburger

2   pounds ground beef
1/2   cup finely chopped green
        bell pepper
1/4   cup finely chopped green onions
3   garlic cloves, chopped

2   tablespoons barbecue sauce
2   teaspoons hot sauce
1   teaspoon dried oregano
    Salt and pepper to taste
6   buns, toasted

Mix the ground beef, green bell pepper, green onions, garlic, barbecue sauce, hot sauce, oregano, salt and pepper in a bowl. Shape into six patties. Grill to 160 degrees on a meat thermometer. Serve on the toasted buns.

SERVES 6

Spaghetti Pie

6   ounces uncooked spaghetti
2   tablespoons butter or margarine
1/3   cup grated Parmesan cheese
2   eggs, beaten
1   cup ricotta cheese
1   pound lean ground beef
1/2   cup chopped onion
1/4   cup chopped green bell pepper

1   (8-ounce) can tomatoes, chopped
1   (6-ounce) can tomato paste
1   teaspoon sugar
1   teaspoon dried oregano, crushed
1/2   teaspoon garlic salt
1/2   cup (2 ounces) shredded
        mozzarella cheese

Cook the spaghetti using the package directions; drain. There should be about 3 1/2 cups cooked spaghetti. Combine with the butter in a bowl. Add the Parmesan cheese and eggs and mix well. Place in a buttered 10-inch pie plate and shape to form a pie shell. Spread the ricotta cheese over the bottom of the shell.

Cook the ground beef with the onion and green bell pepper in a skillet, stirring until the ground beef is brown and crumbly and the vegetables are tender; drain any excess drippings. Stir in the undrained tomatoes, tomato paste, sugar, oregano and garlic salt. Cook until heated through. Spoon into the prepared pie plate.

Bake at 350 degrees for 20 minutes. Sprinkle with the mozzarella cheese and bake for 5 minutes longer or until the cheese melts.

SERVES 6 TO 8

Rack of Spring Lamb à la Provençal with Roasted Tomato Jus

André Poirot, *Executive Chef of The Peabody Little Rock*

1¹/2	cups fine fresh bread crumbs	3	(8-rib, 1¹/2-pound) Frenched
3	tablespoons finely chopped fresh		racks of lamb, trimmed of all
	flat-leaf parsley		but a thin layer of fat
1	tablespoon finely chopped		Salt and pepper to taste
	fresh thyme	1	tablespoon olive oil
1¹/2	teaspoons minced fresh rosemary	2	tablespoons Dijon mustard
1	teaspoon chopped garlic	10	Roma tomatoes, cut into quarters
¹/2	teaspoon salt	2	small onions, cut into wedges
¹/4	teaspoon pepper	1	cup dry white wine
2¹/2	tablespoons olive oil	1	teaspoon chopped garlic

*M*ix the bread crumbs, parsley, thyme, rosemary, 1 teaspoon garlic, ¹/2 teaspoon salt and ¹/4 teaspoon pepper in a bowl. Add 2¹/2 tablespoons olive oil and toss to mix well.

Season the lamb with salt and pepper to taste. Heat 1 tablespoon olive oil in a large heavy skillet over medium-high heat until hot but not smoking. Add the lamb one rack at a time and brown each for 4 minutes, turning once. Spread the fatty sides of each rack with 2 teaspoons of the Dijon mustard and then press the bread crumb mixture gently into the mustard coating on the lamb.

Place the tomatoes and onions in a heavy roasting pan. Place the lamb racks in the pan and roast at 400 degrees for 20 minutes or to 130 degrees on a meat thermometer for medium-rare. Remove to a cutting board and let stand for 10 minutes.

Drain the fat from the roasting pan and place the pan over high heat. Add the wine to the pan and bring to a simmer, stirring any browned bits up from the bottom of the pan. Add 1 teaspoon garlic and cook until slightly reduced and thickened. Adjust the seasoning.

Cut the racks of lamb into chops and serve with the roasted tomato jus.

SERVES 8

Partners for Hope

Entering the work force for the first time ever or the first time in twenty years can be a difficult, if not seemingly impossible, task. JLLR assists with addressing issues facing women transitioning from welfare to the work force. JLLR volunteers work as mentors, conducting mock interviews, fielding questions, and even providing proper interview attire. The women emerge from the program with the renewed confidence to face the future. This program supports our League's mission of developing the potential of women.

Lamb Shanks with Garlic Mashed Potatoes and Haricots Verts

Scott Holtzhouser, *Executive Chef/Owner of Crew*

2	tablespoons olive oil	5¹/2 cups red wine	
1	pound onions, chopped	5	cups lamb stock or veal stock
1	pound carrots, chopped	2	bay leaves
1	pound celery, chopped	6	(12- to 16-ounce) lamb shanks
5	garlic cloves, chopped		Salt and pepper to taste
4	large shallots, chopped		All-purpose flour for dusting
2	tablespoons chopped	2	tablespoons olive oil
	fresh rosemary		Haricots Verts (page 87)
1¹/2	tablespoons tomato paste		Garlic Mashed Potatoes (below)

Heat 2 tablespoons olive oil in a heavy large Dutch oven over high heat. Add the onions, carrots, celery, garlic and shallots and sauté until brown. Add the rosemary and sauté until aromatic. Add the tomato paste and cook for 5 to 7 minutes, stirring constantly and scraping the browned bits up from the bottom of the pan. Add the wine, lamb stock and bay leaves and bring to a boil. Reduce the heat and cover. Maintain at a simmer.

Season the lamb with salt and pepper and dust with flour. Heat 2 tablespoons olive oil in a heavy large skillet over high heat. Add the lamb shanks in batches and sear until brown on all sides; remove to the simmering lamb stock mixture as they brown. Bring to a boil and reduce the heat. Simmer, covered, until the lamb is very tender and nearly falling off the bone.

Remove the lamb to a plate. Remove and discard the bay leaves and cook the remaining liquid until reduced to sauce consistency. Strain and season with salt and pepper. Serve the lamb with the sauce, Garlic Mashed Potatoes and Haricots Verts.

SERVES 6

Garlic Mashed Potatoes

10	garlic cloves	¹/2	cup (1 stick) butter
1	cup olive oil	1	cup half-and-half
4	large Yukon gold potatoes, peeled and coarsely chopped		Salt and pepper to taste

Bring the garlic to a boil in the olive oil in a saucepan. Reduce the heat and simmer until the garlic is golden brown. Remove the garlic and mash with a fork. Reserve the garlic oil for another use.

Boil the potatoes in enough water to cover in a saucepan until tender; drain. Heat the butter with the half-and-half in a saucepan. Combine the potatoes, butter mixture and garlic in a mixing bowl and whip until smooth. Season with salt and pepper.

SERVES 6

Haricots Verts

50   *haricots verts (French green beans)*
$^1/_2$ *cup salt*
1   *shallot, minced*
1   *garlic clove, minced*
$^1/_2$ *cup (1 stick) butter*
    Salt and pepper to taste

Add the beans and salt to enough boiling water to cover in a saucepan. Sauté the shallot and garlic in the butter in a sauté pan. Drain the beans and combine with the shallot mixture in a serving bowl; season with salt and pepper.

SERVES 6

Pork Tenderloin

$^1/_4$ *cup olive oil*
$^1/_4$ *cup honey*
2   *teaspoons finely chopped fresh rosemary*
2   *tablespoons mustard seeds*
2   *teaspoons kosher salt*
1   *tablespoon pepper*
2   *pork tenderloins*

Combine the olive oil, honey, rosemary, mustard seeds, kosher salt and pepper in a bowl and mix well. Add the pork and marinate, covered, in the refrigerator for 4 hours or longer. Drain, reserving the marinade.

Brown the pork on all sides in an ovenproof skillet. Add the reserved marinade. Roast at 350 degrees for 20 to 30 minutes or to 145 to 150 degrees on a meat thermometer. Let stand at room temperature for 7 to 10 minutes. Slice on the diagonal. Serve with cheese grits and a green salad.

SERVES 8

Chili and Sugared Pork Tenderloin

2	pork tenderloins	1	cup sugar
	Olive oil		Salt to taste
1	cup chili powder		

*P*lace the pork in a deep pan. Add enough olive oil to coat well, turning to cover evenly. Add the chili powder and turn to coat well, pressing the chili powder evenly onto all sides. Repeat the process with the sugar. Season lightly on all sides with salt. Marinate, covered, in the refrigerator for 8 hours, if desired.

Grill to 160 degrees on a meat thermometer; the marinade should form a caramelized and blackened crust. Let stand for 20 to 30 minutes before slicing to serve.

SERVES 6 TO 8

Pork Marsala

3	pork tenderloins	3	tablespoons chopped green onions
	All-purpose flour for coating	3	tablespoons chopped parsley
	Vegetable oil for sautéing	2	cups beef broth
2 to 3	tablespoons butter	1/2	cup marsala
8	ounces (or more) mushrooms, sliced		Paprika, salt and pepper to taste

*C*ut the tenderloins into 1/2-inch slices; pound the slices lightly. Sprinkle lightly with flour. Sauté in a small amount of vegetable oil in a skillet over high heat until brown. Remove to a baking dish.

Melt the butter in the skillet and add the mushrooms. Sauté for 5 minutes. Add the green onions, parsley, beef broth, wine, paprika, salt and pepper. Simmer for 5 minutes. Pour over the pork and bake at 350 degrees for 30 minutes.

SERVES 8

Stuff the Bus

Stuff the Bus was created in 2006 by the Junior League of Little Rock to improve the learning experiences of Little Rock children. A child cannot adequately learn without the basic educational supplies, such as paper and pencils. Yet some children go to school every day without such essentials. Stuff the Bus supplies students with a new backpack brimming with the tools they will need throughout their year of learning. This can improve self-esteem and make the child excited for a new school day. We are adding schools annually—beginning with those most in need.

Farmers' Market Supper

Fatoush Salad

69

Chili and Sugared Pork Tenderloin

88

Off-the-Cob Creamed Corn

140

Rivermarket Squash Cakes

152

Tomato Pie

153

Grilled Vegetables

154

Peaches and Basil with Ice Cream

229

Wine: Albarino

Calypso Pork Loin Roast

1	(2-pound) boneless pork loin roast, rolled and tied	1	bay leaf
1	cup packed brown sugar	1	teaspoon salt
2	tablespoons dark rum	$1/2$	teaspoon pepper
2	garlic cloves, minced	$1/2$	cup chicken stock
2	teaspoons ground ginger	$1/4$	cup light rum
$1/2$	teaspoon ground cloves	1	tablespoon all-purpose flour
		$1/4$	cup lime juice

*P*lace the pork roast in a roasting pan. Roast at 375 degrees for $1^1/2$ hours or to 160 degrees on a meat thermometer. Increase the oven temperature to 450 degrees.

Mix the brown sugar, dark rum, garlic, ginger, cloves, bay leaf, salt and pepper to a paste in a bowl. Remove the string from the roast. Spread the paste over the roast. Return to the roasting pan and roast for 8 minutes. Remove to a serving platter.

Place the roasting pan over medium heat. Add the chicken stock and light rum. Bring to a boil, scraping the browned bits up from the bottom of the pan. Sprinkle the flour into the pan and whisk until smooth. Bring to a boil and cook until thickened, whisking constantly. Add the lime juice and cook for 2 minutes. Discard the bay leaf and spoon the sauce into a serving bowl. Serve with the sliced roast.

SERVES 4

Spinach-Stuffed Pork Loin

1	(4-pound) pork loin roast	1	tablespoon olive oil
$1/2$	cup each soy sauce and sherry	8	ounces baby spinach, coarsely chopped
1	tablespoon dry mustard		
$1/2$	teaspoon pepper	$1^1/2$	cups (6 ounces) crumbled blue cheese
8	ounces fresh mushrooms, sliced		
4	garlic cloves, minced	$1/2$	teaspoon each salt and pepper

*B*utterfly the pork, cutting to within 1 inch of the bottom. Open to lie flat in a large dish. Combine the soy sauce, sherry, dry mustard and $1/2$ teaspoon pepper in a bowl and mix well. Pour over the pork. Marinate in the refrigerator for 2 hours.

Sauté the mushrooms with the garlic in the olive oil in a skillet over medium-high heat for 2 to 3 minutes. Mix with the spinach and cheese in a bowl. Drain the pork and spread the spinach mixture over the cut sides of the pork. Replace the sides and secure the roast at $1^1/2$-inch intervals with kitchen twine. Season with the salt and $1/2$ teaspoon pepper.

Place seam side up on a rack in a shallow roasting pan. Roast at 325 degrees for 3 hours or to 160 degrees on a meat thermometer. Let stand for 10 minutes before slicing to serve.

SERVES 8 TO 10

Grilled Pork Chops with Arkansas Black Apples, Turnips and Greens

Lee Richardson, *Executive Chef of Capital Hotel*

GREENS
4 ounces bacon, chopped
2 tablespoons extra-virgin olive oil
$^1/4$ cup ($^1/2$ stick) unsalted butter
2 yellow onions, chopped
1 teaspoon pepper
$^1/4$ cup plus $^1/2$ tablespoon
    brown sugar
$^1/4$ cup apple cider vinegar
2 pounds turnip greens,
    stems removed
1 teaspoon kosher salt

BLACK APPLES
4 Arkansas black apples
1 tablespoon unsalted butter
2 bay leaves

2 cinnamon sticks
2 whole anise
2 tablespoons extra-virgin olive oil
1 teaspoon kosher salt
2 turns freshly cracked pepper

TURNIPS
2 pounds turnips, peeled
2 tablespoons extra-virgin olive oil
1 teaspoon kosher salt
2 turns freshly cracked pepper
1 tablespoon unsalted butter
2 yellow onions, chopped

PORK CHOPS
8 pork chops
    Salt and pepper to taste

Sauté the bacon in the olive oil and butter in a large skillet. Add the onions and pepper and sauté until the onions are caramelized. Add the brown sugar and cook just until it begins to stick. Stir in the vinegar and cook until most of the liquid has evaporated. Add the greens gradually, seasoning with the kosher salt and cooking down before adding more. Cook, covered, over low heat until tender, adding liquid as needed and testing the balance of sour, sweet and salt. You may also cook the greens in a slow oven for several hours; keep warm.

Peel and core the apples and cut into $^1/2$-inch wedges; place in acidulated water. Melt the butter in a skillet over medium heat. Add the bay leaves, cinnamon sticks and anise. Sauté until fragrant. Drain the apples, coat lightly with the olive oil and season with the kosher salt and pepper. Add to the skillet and toss gently to coat. Spoon into a roasting pan and roast at 375 degrees for 20 minutes; remove and discard the bay leaves and spices and keep warm.

Chop the turnips into pieces about half the size of the apple pieces. Coat with the olive oil and season with the kosher salt and pepper. Sauté in the butter in a skillet over medium-high heat just until they begin to shine. Add the onions and cook until the turnips are light brown. Spoon into a roasting pan and roast at 375 degrees for 10 minutes; keep warm.

Season the pork chops with salt and pepper. Grill over cherry wood smoke until cooked through. Combine the turnips and apples in a bowl and mix gently. Serve the turnip greens and the apple and turnip mixture with the pork chops.

SERVES 8

Pork Chops with Apples

1/2   cup all-purpose flour
1   teaspoon paprika
1/2   teaspoon garlic salt
1/2   teaspoon celery salt
1/2   teaspoon seasoned salt
6   (1-inch) pork chops
2   tablespoons olive oil
1   green bell pepper, thinly sliced
3   red apples, thinly sliced
1/2   cup water
1   tablespoon brown sugar
2   tablespoons Worcestershire sauce
     Hot cooked brown rice

Mix the flour, paprika, garlic salt, celery salt and seasoned salt in a 1-gallon sealable plastic bag. Add the pork chops two at a time and shake to coat evenly. Heat the olive oil in a skillet over medium-high heat. Add the pork chops and brown on both sides.

Reduce the heat and add the green bell pepper and apples to the skillet. Mix the water, brown sugar and Worcestershire sauce in a small bowl. Add to the skillet. Simmer, covered, over low heat for 40 to 45 minutes or until the pork chops are tender and cooked through and the sauce is reduced to the desired consistency. Serve over hot cooked brown rice.

SERVES 6

Braised Pork Ribs

RIBS

2   racks pork loin back ribs
2   tablespoons Creole seasoning
3   large onions, sliced
8   garlic cloves, crushed
1   cup Worcestershire sauce
3   tablespoons soy sauce
1¹/3 cups packed brown sugar
3   whole serrano chiles, or to taste
¹/3 cup kosher salt
2   teaspoons red pepper flakes

CHEESE GRITS

3   cups milk
1¹/2 cups chicken stock
1   cup quick-cooking grits
2   cups (8 ounces) shredded
    Cheddar cheese
    Salt and pepper to taste

*S*eason both sides of the ribs with the Creole seasoning. Wrap tightly in plastic wrap and marinate in the refrigerator for 6 hours or longer.

Cut the ribs into 3- to 4-inch portions. Combine with the onions in a large roasting pan. Add the garlic, Worcestershire sauce, soy sauce, brown sugar, serrano chiles, kosher salt and red pepper flakes. Cover the pan tightly with foil. Roast at 350 degrees for 5 hours or until the meat is falling off the bones.

*B*ring the milk and chicken stock to a boil in a saucepan. Stir in the grits. Reduce the heat to low and simmer for 5 minutes or until thickened. Stir in the cheese and cook until the cheese melts, stirring to mix well. Season with salt and pepper. Serve the ribs over the grits.

SERVES 6 TO 8

Potluck

*In 1989, the JLLR approved a new community service project named Potluck.
This was a concept that would forever change how the community dealt with surplus food
at the end of the evening. The purpose of Potluck is to match establishments
routinely having surplus food with shelters feeding the hungry. Under the name Potluck Food
Rescue, the project operates today as its own entity as it serves the hungry of
Little Rock with the continued help of local restaurants. The innovative endeavor has been so
successful that in 2004, this organization was honored as the "Nonprofit
Business of the Year" by Arkansas Business. In one recent year alone, Potluck served more
than 3.6 million pounds of food that would have otherwise been thrown away.
That's a lot of caring big bites for Little Rock!*

Pancetta Pasta for One or More

3	ounces uncooked spaghetti or whole wheat pasta of choice	2	ounces pancetta, sliced and cooked
1	tablespoon salt	1/4	cup (1 ounce) grated Parmesan cheese
1	tablespoon butter, cut into pieces and softened	1	tablespoon capers
			Kosher salt and pepper to taste

Add the pasta and 1 tablespoon salt to enough boiling water to cover in a saucepan. Cook using the package directions; drain. Return the pasta to the saucepan and add the butter, pancetta, cheese, capers, kosher salt and pepper. Toss to mix well. You can increase this recipe by the number of servings needed to serve more.

SERVES 1

Ozark Fettuccini

1/2	cup (1 stick) unsalted butter	2	tomatoes, seeded and chopped
1	cup heavy cream		Grated Parmesan cheese to taste
2	egg yolks		Salt and freshly cracked pepper to taste
6	ounces smoked Ozark ham, thinly sliced	8	ounces fettuccini, cooked
2	zucchini		

Combine the butter, cream and egg yolks in a saucepan and whisk until smooth. Cook over low heat until the butter melts and the mixture thickens slightly, whisking constantly; do not boil. Add the ham. Use a vegetable peeler to shave the zucchini into the sauce. Add the tomatoes and the desired amount of cheese and cook until the cheese melts. Season with salt. Combine with the pasta in a bowl and add additional cheese and cracked pepper; mix well.

SERVES 4

Whole Wheat Pasta

Consider substituting whole wheat or whole grain pasta for white pasta. With three times the fiber, it is heart-healthy, lower in sugar, and more filling than regular pasta. It is readily available at grocery stores in most varieties and requires only a few more minutes of cooking time before the delicious finished product is ready to be enjoyed.

Lasagna Bolognese

BOLOGNESE SAUCE

1	cup chopped onion
1/2	cup chopped celery
2	garlic cloves, chopped
2	tablespoons butter
1	pound bulk Italian sausage
1	pound ground beef
2	tablespoons olive oil
1/2	cup red wine
2	cups chopped tomatoes
3	tablespoons tomato paste
2	cups beef stock
2	bay leaves
1/2	teaspoon dried oregano
1/2	teaspoon basil
	Salt and pepper to taste

BESCIAMELLA SAUCE

3	tablespoons butter
6	tablespoons all-purpose flour
2	cups milk
1	cup heavy cream
1	teaspoon salt
	Nutmeg to taste

LASAGNA

16	ounces uncooked lasagna noodles
16	ounces (4 cups) shredded mozzarella cheese
1/2	cup (2 ounces) grated Parmesan cheese

Sauté the onion, celery and garlic in the butter in a skillet over low heat until golden brown. Remove to a heavy 3- to 4-quart saucepan. Sauté the sausage and ground beef in the olive oil in the skillet, stirring until crumbly and brown; drain any excess drippings. Add the wine and cook until most of the wine has evaporated.

Add the ground beef mixture to the saucepan with the vegetables. Add the tomatoes, tomato paste, beef stock, bay leaves, oregano, basil, salt and pepper. Simmer, partially covered, for 1 hour. Remove and discard the bay leaves.

Melt the butter in a heavy 2- to 3-quart saucepan over low heat. Add the flour and cook for 2 to 3 minutes, stirring constantly. Add the milk and cream gradually and cook until thickened, whisking constantly. Remove from the heat and season with the salt and nutmeg.

Cook the lasagna noodles using the package directions. Drain and rinse in cool water. Drain again on paper towels.

Spread a 1/3-inch layer of the bolognese sauce in a buttered 9×13-inch baking dish. Layer the noodles, the remaining meat sauce, the besciamella sauce and the mozzarella cheese one-third at a time in the prepared pan. Sprinkle with the Parmesan cheese. Bake at 350 degrees for 30 minutes or until bubbly.

SERVES 10

Italian Sausage Pasta

1   pound bulk Italian sausage, casings removed
1   onion, chopped
3 or 4 green onions, chopped
1   red bell pepper, chopped
3 or 4 garlic cloves, minced
1   tablespoon olive oil
2 to 3 cups canned whole or crushed tomatoes
1/4   cup chopped parsley
1   teaspoon oregano
1   teaspoon basil
24   ounces rigatoni, cooked
      Salt and pepper to taste

Sauté the sausage with the onion, green onions, red bell pepper and garlic in the olive oil in a saucepan for 10 to 15 minutes or until the onion is translucent and the sausage is brown and crumbly. Add the tomatoes, parsley, oregano and basil. Simmer for 30 minutes. Combine with the cooked pasta in a bowl and toss to mix well. Season with salt and pepper and serve immediately. You may double this recipe.

SERVES 8 TO 10

Girls Realizing Opportunity Within

After researching the needs of the community, the Junior League of Little Rock found that programs benefiting middle school girls were not widely available. With help from the Little Rock School District, JLLR successfully implemented Girls Realizing Opportunity Within (GROW) in 2004. The mission is to encourage girls to stay in school, make good life choices, and improve their self-image. The Junior League members on the GROW Committee plan monthly educational programs and enrichment field trips. The activities are designed to reach the girls' untapped potential, build self-esteem, and allow them to experience new ideas and skills in a safe, supportive environment. Let's watch these girls and their futures blossom.

New Year's Peas and Sausage

1   pound dried black-eyed peas
8   ounces salt pork
2   pounds smoked sausage
1   pound andouille sausage
3   cups chopped onions
1   bunch green onions, chopped
1   cup chopped parsley
1   cup chopped bell pepper
2   garlic cloves, minced
1   (8-ounce) can tomato sauce
1   tablespoon Worcestershire sauce
1/2   teaspoon hot sauce
1/4   teaspoon dried oregano
1/4   teaspoon dried thyme
1   teaspoon kosher salt
1   teaspoon pepper
    Hot cooked rice

Combine the dried peas with enough water to cover in a bowl. Let stand for 8 hours or longer; drain and rinse. Combine with the salt pork and enough water to cover in a saucepan. Cook, covered, over low heat for 2 hours.

Cut the smoked sausage and andouille sausage into 1/2-inch slices. Brown in batches in a skillet. Remove to a platter, reserving the drippings in the skillet. Add the onions, green onions, parsley, bell pepper and garlic to the drippings in the skillet. Sauté until the vegetables are tender.

Add the sautéed vegetables to the peas in the saucepan. Stir in the tomato sauce, Worcestershire sauce, hot sauce, oregano, thyme, kosher salt and pepper. Cook, covered, for 1 to 2 hours. Add the sausages and cook for 1 hour longer. Serve over hot cooked rice.

SERVES 10

Red Beans and Rice

1	red onion, chopped
1	cup chopped celery
	Chopped tops of 1 bunch green onions
2	garlic cloves, minced
	Olive oil for sautéing
4	(16-ounce) cans dark red kidney beans
1/4	cup ketchup
1/4	cup Worcestershire sauce
1/4	cup dried parsley flakes
1	(15-ounce) can tomato sauce
2	teaspoons sugar
2	tablespoons cider vinegar
1	teaspoon olive oil
2	bay leaves
4	teaspoons chili powder
4	teaspoons seasoning salt
1/4	teaspoon cayenne pepper
1	package smoked link sausage
4	cups hot cooked white rice

Sauté the onion, celery, green onion tops and garlic in a small amount of olive oil in a skillet until tender but not brown. Combine with the undrained beans, ketchup, Worcestershire sauce, parsley flakes, tomato sauce, sugar, vinegar, 1 teaspoon olive oil, the bay leaves, chili powder, seasoning salt and cayenne pepper in a large saucepan. Simmer, covered, for 1 1/2 hours.

Slice the sausage into bite-size pieces. Add to the beans and cook for 30 minutes or until cooked through. Store in the refrigerator for 24 hours to blend the flavors. Reheat and then discard the bay leaves. Serve over the hot cooked rice with corn bread and salad.

SERVES 8

Families and Community Together

The FACT project, Families and Community Together, was adopted by the JLLR in the spring of 2008. The main objective of this initiative is to provide mentoring to the teen parents participating in the Centers for Youth and Families' Young Moms/Dads-Healthy Families program. This effort reaches out to teen moms and dads with support services so they can complete their education, be self-sufficient, and provide the best care possible for their children. The Parent Center, established by JLLR, facilitates this program by supporting the participants with information about parenting, employment, and education. JLLR mentors are proud to foster a positive relationship, knowing that their volunteer time will make a lasting impact on these families and the community.

Family Secret Chicken

1	tablespoon olive oil	1	(4-inch) strip lemon zest with the pith removed
1/2	cup dried apricots		
1/4	cup dried sour cherries	1/2	cup tawny port
1/2	cup dried figs or prunes	1	small cinnamon stick
2	tablespoons pine nuts	1	cup chicken stock
1	(4-inch) strip orange zest with the pith removed	1	(3 1/2-pound) rotisserie chicken, cut into 8 pieces

Heat the olive oil in a large Dutch oven over medium heat. Add the apricots, cherries, figs, pine nuts, orange zest and lemon zest. Sauté for 3 to 5 minutes or until the pine nuts are golden brown and the fruits begin to brown. Add the wine and cinnamon stick and cook for 5 minutes or until syrupy. Add the chicken stock and any juices from the chicken. Increase the heat and bring to a boil. Cook for 5 minutes or until the liquid is reduced.

Add the chicken and spoon the liquid and fruit over the chicken, scraping the browned bits up from the bottom of the Dutch oven. Bake, covered, at 425 degrees for 10 minutes or until the chicken is heated through. Remove and discard the orange zest, lemon zest and cinnamon stick. Serve with cooked rice or couscous.

You may add dried cranberries, currents or pistachios to vary the recipe, which takes only about 30 minutes to prepare, but tastes as if has been cooking all day.

SERVES 4

Lemon Chicken Pasta

3/4	cup olive oil	1/2	cup chopped fresh basil
1	garlic clove, minced	16	ounces linguini, cooked and drained
	Grated zest and juice of 2 lemons		
3	ounces fresh baby spinach, chopped	1	lemon pepper rotisserie chicken, boned and chopped
1	cup (4 ounces) grated Parmesan cheese		Kosher salt and freshly ground pepper to taste

Combine the olive oil, garlic and lemon zest in a small bowl. Squeeze the lemon juice over the spinach in a large bowl. Add the cheese and basil and toss to mix well. Add the hot pasta and the olive oil mixture and mix well.

Add the chicken and season with kosher salt and pepper. Serve with a light white wine and a sliced baguette drizzled with olive oil and sprinkled with pepper.

SERVES 8

Boursin Chicken

Jason Knapp, *Executive Chef of The Governor's Mansion*

5 ounces Boursin Cheese, softened (below)	1 cup seasoned bread crumbs
1 tablespoon all-purpose flour	1/2 cup (2 ounces) grated Parmesan cheese
1/4 cup shredded carrots	1/2 cup chopped flat-leaf parsley
1/4 cup chopped pecans	1/2 cup (1 stick) butter, melted
8 boneless skinless chicken breasts	

Combine the Boursin Cheese with the flour, carrots and pecans in a bowl. Place the chicken between layers of waxed paper and pound until moderately thin. Spread the cheese mixture on the chicken and roll the chicken to enclose the filling, securing with wooden picks.

Mix the bread crumbs, Parmesan cheese and parsley in a bowl. Dip the chicken rolls in the melted butter and coat with the bread crumb mixture. Place seam side down in a 9×13-inch baking dish. Bake at 350 degrees for 1 hour.

SERVES 8

Boursin Cheese

8 ounces cream cheese, softened	1/2 teaspoon basil
1/2 cup (1 stick) butter, softened	1/2 teaspoon parsley
1/2 teaspoon dill weed	1/4 teaspoon garlic salt

Combine the cream cheese, butter, dill weed, basil, parsley and garlic salt in a food processor and process until smooth. Chill in the refrigerator. Shape as desired.

MAKES 1 1/2 CUPS

Holiday House

November in Little Rock means Holiday House, the three-day shopping event of the season. With more than one hundred merchants, looking for the hard-to-find gift has never been so easy. But just remember this: it's not all about the shopping. This fund-raising event is about giving. The proceeds from Holiday House help the Junior League of Little Rock's community projects spread joy year-round.

Chicken and Dumplings

6   (14-ounce) cans chicken broth
3 or 4 bay leaves
    Salt and black pepper to taste
2 to 4 teaspoons lemon pepper, or
    to taste
2 to 4 teaspoons cayenne pepper,
    or to taste
2   tablespoons all-purpose flour
3 or 4 garlic cloves, chopped
    Olive oil for sautéing
8   boneless skinless chicken breasts
    Cavender's seasoning and Cajun
    seasoning to taste

1   large yellow onion,
    coarsely chopped
1   bunch carrots, peeled and
    coarsely chopped
1   bunch celery, coarsely chopped
3 or 4 garlic cloves, chopped
6 to 8 cans refrigerator biscuits,
    chilled (do not use
    butter-flavor biscuits)
    Basil to taste
1 to 2 cups heavy cream,
    at room temperature

Combine the chicken broth, bay leaves, salt, black pepper, lemon pepper and cayenne pepper in a stockpot. Add enough water to fill the stockpot two-thirds full and bring to a boil. Reduce the heat and maintain at a simmer. Remove 2 to 4 tablespoons of the boiling chicken broth to a bowl. Whisk in the flour, blending until smooth; set aside.

Sauté 3 or 4 garlic cloves in a small amount of olive oil in a large skillet. Season the chicken with Cavender's seasoning and Cajun seasoning. Add to the skillet and sauté for 10 minutes on each side; reduce the heat to low to medium-low and cook until the chicken is slightly pink, cutting into the chicken to check the degree of doneness; the chicken will continue to cook in the hot broth. Remove from the heat. Remove the chicken to a plate when it is cooked through.

Cut the chicken into bite-size pieces, discarding the bones and fat. Sauté the onion, carrots, celery and 3 or 4 garlic cloves in the drippings in the skillet until the vegetables are golden brown.

Return the chicken broth mixture to a boil. Open one can of biscuits at a time and separate the biscuits. Divide each biscuit into four pieces and drop enough of the biscuits into the boiling broth so that the top of the broth is covered with floating biscuits. Cook until the biscuits begin to sink, stirring occasionally. Add additional biscuits and cook until each addition sinks; reduce the heat to medium about halfway through the process, occasionally stirring the bottom of the saucepan gently to prevent scorching.

Add the chopped chicken and sautéed vegetables with the drippings from the skillet to the stockpot. Season with basil and adjust the salt and black pepper. Reduce the heat to low. Blend in the flour mixture, stirring to mix well. Simmer for 15 minutes or until thickened, stirring until smooth. Add the desired amount of cream gradually, stirring constantly. Simmer for 15 to 30 minutes or until of the desired consistency, stirring occasionally. Remove and discard the bay leaves. Serve immediately or reheat to serve the next day.

SERVES 8

Chicken in Orange Sauce with Mushrooms

4   *large boneless skinless chicken breasts*
     Salt and pepper to taste
1/2 *cup (1 stick) butter*
8   *ounces portobello mushrooms,*
     cut into quarters
1/2 *cup chopped onion*
1   *tablespoon thawed frozen orange*
     juice concentrate
1/2 *cup chicken broth*
1   *cup white wine*

Season the chicken with salt and pepper. Brown in the butter in a large skillet. Remove to a baking sheet. Bake at 350 degrees for 15 to 20 minutes or until cooked through.

Sauté the mushrooms with the onion in the drippings in the skillet until the onion is translucent. Add the orange juice concentrate, chicken broth and wine and cook over medium heat until reduced by one-half. Pour over the chicken and serve immediately. This is very good served with rice.

SERVES 4

Poultry Brine

The process of brining is the secret to moist and tender poultry. This brine can be used for chicken and turkey. To prepare the brine, heat one gallon of water in a large stockpot over medium-high heat. Add one and one-half cups packed brown sugar, one cup of kosher salt, two bay leaves, and two tablespoons each of cayenne pepper, dried thyme, dried oregano, and dried basil. Mix until the salt and sugar are dissolved. Let cool, adding ice cubes if necessary. Place the chicken or turkey in the brine and chill in the refrigerator for 24 to 48 hours.

Hong Kong Chicken

Kathy Webb, *Executive Chef/Co-Owner of Lilly's Dim Sum, Then Some*
Nancy Tesmer, *Co-Owner of Lilly's Dim Sum, Then Some*

HONG KONG SAUCE

1	(13-ounce) can coconut milk
1/3	cup creamy peanut butter
1	tablespoon soy sauce (Yamasa or Kikkoman soy sauce)
2	tablespoons sesame oil
1	tablespoon fresh lime juice
1	tablespoon honey
1/3	cup grated fresh ginger
1	teaspoon chopped fresh cilantro
1/3	teaspoon crushed red pepper flakes

CHICKEN

12 to 16	ounces uncooked angel hair pasta
3	tablespoon soy sauce
2	tablespoons sugar
1	pound boneless skinless chicken breasts, cut into 1-inch pieces
	Vegetable oil for stir-frying
12 to 14	thin slices white mushrooms
12 to 14	thin (3-inch) slices red bell peppers
1	teaspoon minced garlic
1/4	cup chopped scallions

Whisk the coconut milk, peanut butter, soy sauce, sesame oil, lime juice and honey in a bowl until smooth. Whisk in the ginger, cilantro and red pepper flakes. Store in the refrigerator.

Cook the pasta in boiling water to cover in a stockpot for 12 to 15 minutes. Drain and rinse with cold water; cool. Chill, covered, in the refrigerator.

Combine the soy sauce and sugar in a bowl. Add the chicken and turn to coat well. Marinate, covered, in the refrigerator for 2 to 3 hours.

Heat enough vegetable oil to cover the bottom of a wok over medium heat. Add the chicken and stir-fry for 2 to 3 minutes; stir constantly to avoid overbrowning. Remove the chicken from the skillet. Wipe the skillet with a paper towel and add a small amount of vegetable oil.

Add the mushrooms, red bell peppers, garlic and scallions and stir-fry until tender. Add the Hong Kong sauce, chicken and noodles; toss to coat evenly.

SERVES 6

Rosemary Chicken Breasts

1/4 cup lemon juice	Grated zest of 1 orange
1/4 cup Dijon mustard	3 tablespoons chopped
1 teaspoon cracked pepper	fresh rosemary
6 chicken breasts	1 teaspoon poultry seasoning
1/2 cup (1 stick) butter	1 teaspoon kosher salt
3 tablespoons sugar	1/4 cup lemon juice
2 garlic cloves, minced	1 tablespoon Dijon mustard

Combine 1/4 cup lemon juice, 1/4 cup Dijon mustard and the pepper in a bowl and mix well. Add the chicken and turn to coat well. Marinate in the refrigerator for 4 hours or longer; drain and discard the marinade.

Melt the butter in a saucepan. Add the sugar, garlic, orange zest, rosemary, poultry seasoning and kosher salt. Stir in 1/4 cup lemon juice and 1 tablespoon Dijon mustard. Bring to a simmer and simmer for 5 minutes. Pour half the mixture into a bowl and reserve.

Grill the chicken over medium heat until cooked through and the juices run clear, basting every 2 to 3 minutes with the remaining rosemary mixture. Spoon the reserved sauce over the chicken to serve.

SERVES 6

Chicken Piccata

4 boneless skinless chicken breasts	Juice of 1 lemon
Salt and pepper to taste	2 tablespoons butter
1 cup all-purpose flour	2 tablespoons capers, drained
2 tablespoons olive oil	3 tablespoons chopped flat-leaf
2 tablespoons butter	Italian parsley
1 splash of white wine	Hot cooked angel hair pasta

Season the chicken with salt and pepper; coat with the flour. Heat the olive oil and 2 tablespoons butter in a large skillet or sauté pan. Add the chicken and sauté for 5 minutes on each side or until golden brown. Remove the chicken to a platter.

Add the wine to the skillet and stir the browned bits up from the bottom of the skillet. Add the lemon juice and 2 tablespoons butter. Simmer until thickened and bubbly, stirring frequently. Return the chicken to the skillet and add the capers and parsley. Cook until heated through. Serve over hot cooked angel hair pasta.

SERVES 4

Wild and Cheesy Chicken Casseroles

Judy Adams, *Owner of Catering to You*

1/4 cup chopped onion
1/4 cup chopped green bell pepper
1 (6-ounce) can mushrooms
1/2 cup (1 stick) butter
1/2 cup milk
1/2 cup chicken broth
2 (10-ounce) cans cream of chicken soup
4 cups (16 ounces) chopped Velveeta cheese
2 cups (8 ounces) shredded Cheddar cheese

1 (2-ounce) jar chopped pimento
3 packages long grain and wild rice mix, cooked (tested with Uncle Ben's)
6 cups chopped cooked chicken
1 (8-ounce) can water chestnuts, drained
1/2 cup (2 ounces) shredded Cheddar cheese

Sauté the onion, green bell pepper and mushrooms in the butter in a saucepan until tender. Add the milk, chicken broth, soup, Velveeta cheese and 2 cups Cheddar cheese. Cook over medium heat until the cheeses melt, stirring to blend well. Remove from the heat and add the pimento, rice, chicken and water chestnuts; mix well. Spoon into two greased 9×13-inch baking dishes. Cover with foil and bake at 350 degrees for 40 minutes. Sprinkle with 1/2 cup Cheddar cheese and bake, uncovered, until the cheese on top melts. Serve hot.

SERVES 12 TO 14

Bow Tie Chicken Pasta

8 boneless skinless chicken tenderloins
2 teaspoons Cajun seasoning
2 tablespoon butter
3 green onions, thinly sliced
6 ounces mushrooms, thinly sliced
2 cups heavy cream
1/4 teaspoon dried basil

1/8 teaspoon garlic powder
1/4 teaspoon salt
1/8 teaspoon freshly ground pepper
7 ounces sun-dried tomatoes, chopped
6 ounces bow tie pasta, cooked al dente
Grated Parmesan cheese to taste

Cut each chicken tenderloin into two pieces. Combine with the Cajun seasoning in a bowl and toss to coat well. Sauté the chicken in the butter in a large skillet over medium heat for 5 to 7 minutes or until tender.

Reduce the heat and add the green onions, mushrooms, cream, basil, garlic powder, salt and pepper. Cook until heated through. Add the sun-dried tomatoes and pasta. Sprinkle with cheese; mix well. Remove from the heat and let stand for 5 to 10 minutes or until thickened before serving.

SERVES 4

Chilaquiles

1¹/2 tablespoons olive oil
2   onions, chopped
2   garlic cloves, minced
1   (28-ounce) can tomatoes, finely chopped
1   (16-ounce) can kidney beans, drained
1   (16-ounce) can chopped green chiles, drained
1¹/2 cups chopped cooked chicken (optional)
12   corn tortillas, cut into 2-inch strips
1   cup sour cream
2¹/2 cups (10 ounces) shredded Monterey Jack cheese

Heat the olive oil in a skillet over medium-high heat. Add the onions and garlic and sauté for 10 minutes or until tender. Stir in the undrained tomatoes, kidney beans, green chiles and chicken. Cook for 5 minutes or until slightly thickened, stirring occasionally.

Spread half the mixture in a 9×13-inch baking dish and top with half the tortilla strips. Layer half the sour cream and half the cheese over the tortilla strips. Layer the remaining tortilla strips, remaining chicken mixture, remaining sour cream and remaining cheese in the dish. Bake at 350 degrees for 35 minutes or until bubbly and heated through.

SERVES 4

Nightingales

Perhaps one of the most stressful times for a parent is caring for a child during a hospital stay. Since 1999, the JLLR has provided a broad variety of upbeat activities and personal care services to the parents and caregivers of children who are patients at Arkansas Children's Hospital and University of Arkansas Medical Sciences Family Home. The Nightingales program provides a needed break for parents in the form of relaxing moments, a snack break, or a friendly game. JLLR smiles can be great medicine!

Apricot Ginger Cornish Hens

2 tablespoons orange marmalade
3/4 cup apricot preserves
1 tablespoon fresh orange juice
1 tablespoon fresh lemon juice
1 tablespoon minced fresh ginger
4 Cornish game hens
2 teaspoons salt
1 tablespoon freshly ground pepper
1/2 cup slivered almonds
2 tablespoons butter
2 tablespoons olive oil
1/2 cup chopped shallots
1 (6-ounce) package wild rice mix
2 1/3 cups chicken broth

Melt the orange marmalade in a small saucepan over low heat. Press through a strainer. Combine the strained syrup with the apricot preserves, orange juice, lemon juice and ginger in a bowl; mix well.

Remove the giblet package from the hens and tuck the wing tips under the backs. Secure the legs with kitchen twine and sprinkle with the salt and pepper.

Place breast side up on a rack in a roasting pan. Roast at 350 degrees for 45 minutes. Brush with one-third of the apricot preserves mixture. Roast for 30 to 45 minutes longer or until the juices run clear when the hens are pierced with a fork, basting occasionally with half the remaining apricot mixture.

Sauté the almonds in the butter and olive oil in a skillet until light brown. Remove the almonds to a bowl with a slotted spoon. Add the shallots to the drippings in the skillet and sauté over medium-high heat until tender. Add the rice mix, contents of the seasoning packet and the chicken broth and bring to a boil.

Reduce the heat and simmer, covered, for 25 minutes or until the rice is tender and the liquid has been absorbed. Stir in the almonds. Spoon onto serving plates. Arrange the hens over the rice. Heat the remaining apricot sauce in a saucepan and brush over the hens to serve.

SERVES 4

Smothered Dove with Pan Gravy

12 to 16 dove breasts, cleaned
  Granulated garlic, hot sauce, salt
  and black pepper to taste
1 cup all-purpose flour
  Cayenne pepper to taste
3/4 cup vegetable oil
1/4 cup all-purpose flour
2 cups chopped white onions

1 cup chopped red bell pepper
1/2 cup chopped celery
1/4 cup minced garlic
2 1/2 to 3 cups chicken stock
1 cup sliced green onion tops
1/4 cup chopped parsley
  Hot cooked wild rice

Combine the dove with granulated garlic, hot sauce, salt and black pepper in a bowl. Marinate, covered, in the refrigerator for 2 hours or longer. Drain, discarding the marinade.

Season 1 cup flour with granulated garlic, salt, black pepper and cayenne pepper in a sealable plastic bag. Add the dove and shake to coat well, shaking off any excess flour. Heat the oil in a cast-iron Dutch oven over medium-high heat. Add the dove and sauté until brown on all sides. Remove to a plate.

Stir 1/4 cup flour into the drippings in the Dutch oven. Cook until light brown, whisking constantly. Add the onions, red bell pepper, celery and minced garlic and sauté for 3 to 5 minutes or until the vegetables are tender.

Return the dove to the Dutch oven and add 2 1/2 cups chicken stock gradually. Bring to a boil and reduce the heat. Cook until thickened, whisking constantly. Simmer, covered, for 45 to 60 minutes or until the dove are tender, adding additional chicken stock as needed.

Remove from the heat and stir in the green onion tops and parsley. Cook, covered, for 10 minutes longer. Serve over hot cooked wild rice.

SERVES 4

Buckle Up and Be Safe

Buckle Up and Be Safe is a JLLR program designed to help prevent deaths and serious injuries from motor vehicle crashes by educating children and parents about the importance of buckling up for every ride. JLLR volunteers demonstrate the correct way to put a child in a car seat and help parents determine if a child is able to move up to an adult lap-and-shoulder belt. We are glad to be a driving force for safety!

Duck with Wild Rice

8 to 10 duck breasts
    Granulated garlic, salt and pepper to taste
$^1/2$ cup vegetable oil
1   cup chopped white onion
1   cup chopped celery
1   cup chopped mixed red and green bell pepper
$^1/4$ cup minced garlic
1   cup chopped canned tomatoes
1   cup sliced fresh mushrooms
$5^1/2$ cups chicken stock or beef stock
3   cups uncooked wild rice
1   cup sliced green onions
$^1/4$ cup chopped fresh parsley
1   tablespoon chopped fresh basil
1   tablespoon chopped fresh thyme

Season the duck with granulated garlic, salt and pepper. Heat the vegetable oil in a 12-quart cast-iron Dutch oven. Add the duck and cook until brown on both sides. Remove to a platter.

Add the onion, celery, bell pepper and minced garlic to the drippings in the Dutch oven and sauté until tender. Add the tomatoes and mushrooms and sauté for 3 minutes.

Return the duck to the Dutch oven and add the chicken stock. Bring to a boil and reduce the heat. Add the wild rice, green onions, parsley, basil and thyme. Simmer, covered, over low heat for 30 minutes; do not stir. Remove from the heat and fluff with a fork. Let stand, covered, for 10 minutes before serving.

SERVES 8 TO 10

Arkansas Fried Catfish with Crawfish Étouffée

André Poirot, *Executive Chef of The Peabody Little Rock*

1¹/2 cups yellow cornmeal
¹/4   cup all-purpose flour
1   teaspoon garlic powder
1   tablespoon salt
1   teaspoon cayenne pepper

¹/2   teaspoon black pepper
8   catfish fillets
      Vegetable oil for frying
      Crawfish Étouffée (below)

Mix the cornmeal, flour, garlic powder, salt, cayenne pepper and black pepper in a shallow bowl. Add the catfish and coat well, shaking off any excess flour mixture. Heat oil to 375 degrees in a deep fryer. Deep-fry the fish in the heated oil for 3 to 4 minutes on each side or until golden brown. Drain on paper towels. Spoon Crawfish Étouffée over the catfish to serve.

SERVES 8

Crawfish Étouffée

¹/4   cup all-purpose flour
¹/4   cup vegetable oil
¹/2   cup finely chopped white onion
¹/2   cup finely chopped green
      bell pepper
¹/4   cup finely chopped celery
4   garlic cloves, chopped
2   cups fish stock or chicken stock

2   tablespoons tomato paste
1   bay leaf
¹/4   teaspoon dried thyme
      Tabasco sauce, salt and pepper
      to taste
8   ounces crawfish tails, peeled
¹/4   cup finely chopped green onions

Blend the flour into the oil in a sauté pan over medium heat. Cook for 10 to 15 minutes or until light brown, stirring constantly to prevent overbrowning, as this will create a bitter taste.

Add the onion, green bell pepper, celery and garlic and sauté for 3 to 4 minutes. Stir in the fish stock, tomato paste, bay leaf, thyme, Tabasco sauce, salt and pepper; mix well. Cook for 10 minutes. Remove and discard the bay leaf. Add the crawfish tails and green onions. Cook for 1 minute. Adjust the seasoning.

SERVES 4

Macadamia-Crusted Halibut with Pineapple Salsa

PINEAPPLE SALSA
1   (20-ounce) can pineapple
    tidbits, drained
1   cup chopped tomato
1   jalapeño chile, seeded
    and chopped
2   tablespoons chopped cilantro
1/4   cup chopped green onions
    Salt and pepper to taste

HALIBUT
1/2   cup crushed potato chips
1/2   cup chopped macadamia nuts
    or walnuts
1   teaspoon sea salt
4   thick halibut fillets
1   egg, beaten
1/4   cup (1/2 stick) butter

Toss the pineapple, tomato, jalapeño chile, cilantro and green onions gently in a bowl. Season with salt and pepper and mix well. Let stand at room temperature to blend the flavors.

Mix the crushed potato chips with the macadamia nuts and sea salt in a bowl. Dip the fish fillets into the egg and coat with the macadamia nut mixture, pressing to cover well. Melt the butter in a large skillet and add the fillets. Sauté for 3 to 5 minutes on each side or until the fish flakes easily with a fork. Serve with the salsa, a salad and fresh vegetables.

SERVES 4

Bourbon-Lacquered Salmon

1/4   cup packed brown sugar
1/4   cup bourbon
1/4   cup soy sauce
2   tablespoons olive oil
1/2   teaspoon minced garlic

4   (6- to 8-ounce) fresh salmon
    fillets or thawed frozen
    salmon fillets
    Lemon juice and water to taste

Combine the brown sugar, bourbon, soy sauce, olive oil and garlic in a 1-gallon sealable plastic bag. Add the salmon fillets. Press the air out of the bag and seal. Marinate in the refrigerator for 1 hour or longer. Drain, reserving the marinade.

Place the salmon on a grill heated to medium-hot. Grill for 3 to 5 minutes on each side, brushing frequently with some of the reserved marinade.

Heat the remaining marinade in a small saucepan until syrupy. Strain into a bowl and add enough lemon juice and water to reach the desired consistency and flavor. Brush or drizzle on the salmon to serve.

SERVES 4

Island Salmon

4	salmon fillets	4	teaspoons chili powder
1/4	cup pineapple juice	3/4	teaspoon ground cumin
2	tablespoons fresh lemon juice	1/4	teaspoon cinnamon
2	tablespoons brown sugar	1/2	teaspoon salt
2	teaspoons grated lemon zest	1	cedar plank

Cut each salmon fillet into two portions. Combine with the pineapple juice and lemon juice in a large sealable plastic bag and seal. Marinate in the refrigerator for 1 hour.

Mix the brown sugar, lemon zest, chili powder, cumin, cinnamon and salt in a bowl. Drain the salmon and place on a cedar plank. Rub the top of the salmon with the brown sugar mixture. Bake at 375 degrees for 15 to 20 minutes or until the fish flakes easily with a fork.

SERVES 8

Sesame Salmon

SALMON		SESAME GINGER GLAZE	
1/4	cup sugar	2	bunches green onions, chopped
1	teaspoon pepper	2	tablespoons water
4 to 6	(8-ounce) salmon fillets	2	teaspoons soy sauce
1	tablespoon peanut oil	1 1/2	teaspoons sesame oil
1/4	cup soy sauce	1	(1-inch) piece of ginger, peeled
1	tablespoon toasted sesame seeds		and chopped

Mix the sugar and pepper on a plate. Add the salmon and coat well. Heat the peanut oil in a nonstick skillet. Add the salmon and sauté for 5 minutes. Turn the salmon and add the soy sauce to the skillet. Cook, covered, for 5 minutes longer. Place on serving plates and sprinkle with the sesame seeds.

Combine the green onions, water, soy sauce, sesame oil and ginger in a saucepan. Cook until heated through. Serve over the salmon, if desired.

SERVES 4 TO 6

Glazed Sea Bass

1/3   cup mirin
1/3   cup sake
1/3   cup miso paste
2   tablespoons soy sauce
2   tablespoons brown sugar
4   (6-ounce) sea bass fillets

Combine the mirin, sake, miso paste, soy sauce and brown sugar in a bowl. Add the sea bass and marinate in the refrigerator for 2 hours. Drain, reserving some of the marinade.

Place the sea bass in a baking pan lined with foil. Drizzle with the reserved marinade. Broil for 6 minutes.

SERVES 4

Japanese Ingredients

Mirin is a popular Japanese ingredient. It is a rice wine similar to sake but sweeter and lower in alcohol content. It is a great accompaniment to fish, as it removes any unwanted "fishy" flavor. Mirin is readily available in the Asian section of most grocery stores.

Miso paste is a traditional Japanese food made from soybeans and is used frequently in Asian cooking. It is often used as a thickening agent in soups or in sauces or spreads. It can be found in the refrigerator section of most Asian grocery stores and some specialty grocery stores.

Pan-Seared Sea Bass with Pomegranate Crème Fraîche and Roasted Butternut Squash

Donnie Ferneau, *Chef/Owner of Ferneau*

ROASTED BUTTERNUT SQUASH
1/3   cup butter, melted
2   pounds butternut squash, peeled, seeded and chopped
1/2   cup chopped red onion
2   tablespoons brown sugar
1   teaspoon cumin
      Ferneau House Seasoning to taste

POMEGRANATE CRÈME FRAÎCHE
1/2   cup pomegranate juice
1/2   cup sour cream

SEA BASS
4   (6-ounce) portions sea bass
      Ferneau House Seasoning to taste
1   teaspoon olive oil

Mix the butter, squash, onion, brown sugar, cumin and Ferneau House Seasoning in a bowl. Spread in a baking pan sprayed with nonstick cooking spray. Roast at 500 degrees for 12 minutes or until golden brown.

Combine the pomegranate juice and sour cream in a bowl. Mix until smooth.

Season the sea bass with Ferneau House Seasoning. Heat the olive oil in an ovenproof skillet. Add the sea bass skin side up and sear for 2 minutes or until the fish releases from the skillet. Turn the fish and bake at 500 degrees for 4 to 8 minutes or until done to taste. Let stand at room temperature for 2 minutes. Serve with the squash and the crème fraîche.

You can substitute salt and pepper to taste for the Ferneau House Seasoning.

SERVES 4

Crab Meat Imperial

16   ounces fresh lump crab meat, shells
      and cartilage removed
1/2 cup (2 ounces) shredded Cheddar cheese
1/2 cup mayonnaise
1   tablespoon lemon juice
2   tablespoons capers
1/2 teaspoon salt
      Red pepper to taste
      Shredded Cheddar cheese to taste
      Paprika to taste

Combine the crab meat, 1/2 cup cheese, the mayonnaise, lemon juice, capers, salt and red pepper in a bowl and mix gently. Spoon into greased seafood shells and top with additional cheese and paprika. Bake at 350 degrees for 20 minutes.

SERVES 6

Bargain Boutique

Since the 1960s, the JLLR has been operating—through one form or another—its own resale "store" to help fund community projects. In 1962, the Bargain Box was open throughout the week, and all proceeds from merchandise sold were utilized by the League for its civic outreach. In 1978, Bargain Barn opened and became a Little Rock shopping extravaganza for nearly thirty years. Bargain Barn was an annual sale lasting just one day—and what a day it was. Opened in 2006, Bargain Boutique is a day-long consignment sale that offers quality merchandise across a wide range of styles and prices. All flying under the same banner to aid the JLLR cause, Bargain Box, Barn, and Boutique represent opportunities to link up the zeal of the shopper with the comprehensive programs of the League. Thumbs-up for community service!

Seared Sea Scallops with Oven-Roasted Fennel and Tarragon Butter

André Poirot, *Executive Chef of The Peabody Little Rock*

OVEN-ROASTED FENNEL
1   fennel bulb, thinly sliced
1   sweet onion, thinly sliced
1   cup olive oil
    Sea salt and pepper to taste

TARRAGON BUTTER
1   cup (2 sticks) butter, softened
    Juice of 1 lemon
2   teaspoons chopped shallots

1/2   teaspoon chopped garlic
2   tablespoons chopped
    fresh tarragon
    Salt and pepper to taste

SCALLOPS
12   (10- to 15-count) sea scallops
     Salt and pepper to taste
     Olive oil for sautéing

Mix the fennel, onion, olive oil, sea salt and pepper in a bowl. Spread in a baking pan. Roast at 350 degrees for 10 minutes or until lightly caramelized.

Combine the butter with the lemon juice, shallots, garlic, tarragon, salt and pepper in a bowl and mix well.

Season the scallops with salt and pepper. Sauté in a small amount of olive oil in a large skillet until golden brown on both sides. Spoon the fennel into a baking dish. Arrange the scallops over the prepared layer. Top each scallop with 1 teaspoon of the butter, reserving the remaining butter for another use. Bake until the butter is melted and bubbly. Serve immediately.

SERVES 8

Creole Barbecued Shrimp

1/4 cup (1/2 stick) butter
1/4 cup olive oil
1/4 cup ketchup
1/4 cup Worcestershire sauce
1/2 teaspoon Tabasco sauce, or
   to taste
   Juice of 1 lemon
4 garlic cloves, chopped
2 tablespoons Creole seasoning
1 tablespoon chili powder

1 teaspoon paprika
1 teaspoon dried oregano
1 teaspoon dried parsley, or
   1 tablespoon chopped
   fresh parsley
   Cayenne pepper to taste
3/4 cup (6 ounces) beer
2 pounds extra-large shrimp, heads
   removed and in the shells

Combine the butter, olive oil, ketchup, Worcestershire sauce, Tabasco sauce, lemon juice, garlic, Creole seasoning, chili powder, paprika, oregano, parsley and cayenne pepper in a saucepan. Cook over low heat until the butter melts, stirring to mix well. Remove from the heat and stir in the beer. Cool to room temperature.

Spread the shrimp in a foil-lined 9×13-inch baking pan. Pour the sauce over the shrimp. Chill, covered, for 2 hours, stirring every 30 minutes.

Bake, uncovered, at 400 degrees for 12 to 18 minutes or just until the shrimp are pink. Spoon the shrimp and sauce into a bowl and serve with crusty French bread for dipping.

SERVES 4 TO 6

A Finishing Touch

After serving messy finger foods, treat your guests to warm, wet hand towels with lemon. Buy a package of white waffle towels and moisten with one quart of water mixed with the juice of one lemon. Wring out the excess and roll attractively. Arrange the towels in an ovenproof pan and cover tightly with foil. When guests sit for dinner, place the towels in the oven and set on the lowest temperature. Remove at the end of the meal, place on a serving platter garnished with lemon slices, and pass around the table.

Rosemary Shrimp with Smoked Gouda Grits

SMOKED GOUDA GRITS
2¹/2 cups instant grits
1 sprig of rosemary
1¹/4 cups (6 ounces) shredded smoked
    Gouda cheese
1 teaspoon garlic salt
1 teaspoon pepper

ROSEMARY SHRIMP
1 (16-ounce) bottle Italian salad
    dressing (tested with
    Wishbone dressing)

¹/2 cup white wine
3 or 4 tablespoons honey, or to taste
¹/4 cup soy sauce
2 tablespoons chopped garlic
2 teaspoons grated orange zest
1 teaspoon salt
1 teaspoon pepper
1 (10-ounce) package frozen peeled
    deveined shrimp, thawed
6 slices fresh pineapple
    Nutmeg to taste

Cook the grits with the rosemary using the package directions in a saucepan sprayed with nonstick cooking spray. Remove and discard the rosemary. Stir in the cheese and season with garlic salt and pepper. Cook until the cheese melts, stirring constantly. Remove from the heat and cover to keep warm.

Whisk the salad dressing, wine, honey, soy sauce, garlic, orange zest, salt and pepper in a bowl until combined. Combine with the shrimp in a sealable plastic bag and seal. Marinate in the refrigerator for 3 to 24 hours; drain.

Spray a grill with nonstick cooking spray. Grill the shrimp until pink and opaque; remove to a platter. Spray the grill again with nonstick cooking spray. Sprinkle both sides of the pineapple with nutmeg. Place on the grill and grill until marked on both sides.

Spoon the grits onto serving plates. Top with the shrimp and arrange the pineapple on the plate. You can also cook the shrimp on wooden skewers that have been soaked in water in a shallow dish for 30 minutes or longer.

SERVES 6

Elizabeth Prewitt Taylor

The Junior League of Little Rock has special admiration for the late Elizabeth Prewitt Taylor. She was the president of the JLLR from 1924 until 1926 and then went on to serve as the national president of the Junior League, elected in 1934. This energetic leader was a strong advocate of the JLLR's efforts to create the Arkansas Arts Center and, in 1963, the Elizabeth Prewitt Taylor Library was established at the Arkansas Arts Center in her memory.

Southern Shrimp Enchiladas

2 tablespoons butter
16 ounces shrimp, peeled
   and deveined
1/2 cup chopped green onions
2 tomatoes, seeded and chopped
1 recipe Enchilada Sauce (below)

12 flour tortillas
2 cups (8 ounces) shredded
   Monterey Jack cheese
1/2 cup chopped green onions
2 tomatoes, seeded and chopped

Melt the butter in a large skillet over high heat. Add the shrimp and 1/2 cup green onions. Sauté for 2 minutes or until the shrimp are pink, stirring frequently. Stir in 2 tomatoes and half the Enchilada Sauce.

Spread the shrimp mixture by one-third cupfuls on the tortillas. Roll the tortillas to enclose the filling and place seam side down in a 9×13-inch baking pan. Spoon the remaining Enchilada Sauce over the enchiladas.

Bake, covered, at 350 degrees for 30 to 45 minutes or until heated through. Sprinkle with the cheese, 1/2 cup green onions and 2 tomatoes. Bake until the cheese melts.

SERVES 8 TO 10

Enchilada Sauce

1/4 cup (1/2 stick) butter
1 jalapeño chile, chopped
1/2 cup chopped red bell pepper
1/2 cup chopped green bell pepper
1/2 onion, chopped
1 garlic clove, minced
1 teaspoon oregano
1 teaspoon salt

Ground red pepper and white
   pepper to taste
1 cup heavy cream
1/2 cup chicken broth
1 cup (4 ounces) shredded
   Monterey Jack cheese
1/2 cup sour cream

Heat the butter in a large saucepan over medium heat until melted. Add the jalapeño chile, red bell pepper, green bell pepper, onion, garlic and oregano. Sauté until the vegetables are tender. Stir in the salt, red pepper and white pepper.

Add the cream and chicken broth. Bring to a boil. Reduce the heat and simmer for 3 to 4 minutes. Add the cheese and cook until the cheese melts, stirring constantly. Remove from the heat and stir in the sour cream.

SERVES 8 TO 10

Shrimp Pernod

James Hale, *Chef/Owner of Acadia Restaurant*

SHRIMP

1	tablespoon olive oil
6 to 8	large shrimp, peeled and deveined
1	teaspoon kosher salt
1/2	teaspoon cracked pepper
1	large tomato, chopped
1/4	cup Pernod
1/4	cup white wine
1	teaspoon dried basil
1/4	cup (1/2 stick) butter, softened
2	teaspoons all-purpose flour
2	teaspoons minced garlic

ORZO

1/2	cup chicken stock or vegetable stock
1	cup artichoke hearts
	Salt and pepper to taste
1	tablespoon butter, softened
1	cup orzo, cooked
1	garlic clove, minced
2	tablespoons grated Parmesan cheese

Heat the olive oil in a large skillet over medium-high heat. Add the shrimp, kosher salt and pepper. Sauté for 15 seconds on each side. Add the tomato and remove from the heat. Stir in the Pernod carefully and allow to ignite; let the flames subside. Stir in the wine and basil. Simmer over medium heat for 1 minute. Remove from the heat and add the butter, flour and garlic; whisk until smooth.

Combine the chicken stock, artichoke hearts, salt and pepper in a medium skillet. Bring to a boil over medium-high heat. Add the butter, pasta and garlic. Cook until heated through, stirring constantly. Remove from the heat and add the cheese; stir until the cheese melts. Spoon into the center of a large plate and top with the shrimp. Spoon the sauce with the tomato over the shrimp.

SERVES 1 OR 2

KOTA Camp

In 2001, the Junior League of Little Rock began KOTA Camp in conjunction with Camp Aldersgate in Little Rock. The camp brings together special needs children and their siblings and friends without disabilities in a unique experience. This program takes place four times a year—two week-long sessions in the summer and two weekend camps throughout the remaining year. The children look forward to activities such as ice cream socials, archery lessons, dances, fishing, arts and crafts, and canoeing. The camp gives parents time to themselves and gives the children time to be children!

Thai Shrimp with Curried Rice

2   tablespoons olive oil
2   garlic cloves, minced
2   teaspoons peeled minced
     fresh ginger
1   teaspoon grated lime zest
     Juice of 1 lime

1/2 teaspoon dried red pepper
     flakes, crushed
2   sprigs of rosemary
16   jumbo shrimp, peeled
     and deveined
     Curried Rice (page 158)

Combine the olive oil, garlic, ginger, lime zest, lime juice, red pepper flakes and rosemary in a 1-quart sealable plastic bag. Add the shrimp, press out the air and seal. Turn to coat the shrimp evenly. Marinate at room temperature for 15 minutes or in the refrigerator for up to 2 hours; drain.

Soak eight bamboo skewers in water for 30 minutes; drain. Thread four shrimp near the heads onto each wooden skewer and insert a second skewer near the tails to hold the shrimp firm and flat as they grill.

Grill the shrimp for 3 minutes on each side or until cooked through. Serve over Curried Rice.

SERVES 4

Prawns Risotto

4   cups chicken broth
2   cups water
1   small onion, sliced
1   rib celery, chopped
1   bay leaf
16   ounces small prawns, peeled
     with the tails intact
1/4 teaspoon minced garlic
2   tablespoons unsalted butter

1 1/4 cups dry white wine
1/2   cup heavy cream
1   small onion, chopped
1/4   cup (1/2 stick) unsalted butter
2   cups uncooked arborio rice
1/2   cup (2 ounces) grated
       Parmesan cheese
       Salt and pepper to taste

Bring the chicken broth and water to a boil in a saucepan. Add the sliced onion, celery and bay leaf. Cook over low heat for 30 minutes. Strain and return to the saucepan; keep warm.

Sauté the prawns and garlic in 2 tablespoons butter in a skillet for several minutes. Add the wine and cook until the wine evaporates. Stir in the cream and remove from the heat.

Sauté the chopped onion in 1/4 cup butter in a saucepan. Add the rice and sauté for several minutes. Add the heated broth mixture gradually, cooking until the liquid is absorbed after each addition and stirring constantly for a total of about 15 to 20 minutes; the rice should be just covered by the broth as it cooks. Add the prawn mixture and cheese. Season with salt and pepper. Cover and let stand for several minutes. Remove and discard the bay leaf.

SERVES 8

Gnocchi Verde

Scott McGehee, *Chef/Proprietor of Boulevard Bread Company*

2¹/2 cups fresh whole milk ricotta cheese	¹/2 teaspoon grated nutmeg
2 pounds fresh spinach, trimmed	1 teaspoon sea salt
²/3 cup grated Parmigiano-Reggiano cheese	White pepper to taste
	1³/4 cups unbleached all-purpose flour
3 jumbo eggs	Salt to taste

*D*rain the ricotta cheese in a cheesecloth-lined strainer set over a bowl until very dry. Spoon into a large bowl.

Wash the spinach; do not shake off the water. Cook in batches without additional water in a large saucepan until wilted. Drain in a colander and let stand until cool enough to handle. Squeeze out the excess moisture; measure about 2 cups cooked spinach.

Chop the spinach coarsely. Purée in a blender or food processor until very smooth. Add to the ricotta cheese in the bowl. Stir in half the Parmigiano-Reggiano cheese, the eggs, nutmeg, sea salt and white pepper. Add the flour gradually, mixing to form a soft dough that does not stick to the hands. Roll about 1 cup of the dough at a time into a rope 1 inch in diameter. Cut the rope into small pieces.

Bring a large stockpot of salted water to a boil. Add about eight to ten gnocchi at a time with a spoon. Cook until the gnocchi float; drain. Add to your favorite tomato or cream sauce. Sprinkle with the remaining cheese to serve.

SERVES 4

Summer Tomato Sauce

3 large tomatoes, peeled and chopped	10 large fresh basil leaves, finely chopped
¹/2 cup extra-virgin olive oil	1 tablespoon finely chopped fresh oregano, or ¹/2 teaspoon dried oregano
Juice of 1 lemon	
2 garlic cloves, minced	
1 small onion, finely chopped	Freshly ground pepper to taste
Hot sauce to taste	

*C*ombine the tomatoes, olive oil, lemon juice, garlic, onion, hot sauce, basil, oregano and pepper in a bowl; mix well. Let stand for 30 minutes or longer to blend the flavors. Serve with 16 ounces cooked hot or room temperature pasta.

SERVES 4

Vegetarian Lasagna

5 quarts water
1 tablespoon olive oil
10 uncooked lasagna noodles
1 onion, minced
1 garlic clove, minced
1 tablespoon olive oil
16 ounces mushrooms, sliced
16 ounces carrots, sliced
3/4 cup black olives, sliced
1 (15-ounce) can tomato sauce
1 (6-ounce) can tomato paste
1 1/2 teaspoons oregano
1/2 teaspoon salt
1/8 teaspoon freshly ground pepper
1 1/2 teaspoons olive oil
2 cups cottage cheese
2 pounds fresh spinach, cooked and well drained
7 cups (28 ounces) shredded Monterey Jack cheese
2 tablespoons grated Parmesan cheese

*B*ring the water and 1 tablespoon olive oil to a boil in a 2-gallon stockpot. Add the lasagna noodles two or three at a time. Cook for 8 to 10 minutes or until tender; drain. Return to the stockpot and cover with warm water to prevent sticking together.

Sauté the onion and garlic in 1 tablespoon olive oil in a large skillet over medium heat for 2 minutes. Add the mushrooms and sauté for 12 to 15 minutes or until the moisture evaporates. Add the carrots and sauté for 3 to 5 minutes or until tender. Stir in the black olives, tomato sauce, tomato paste, oregano, salt and pepper. Remove from the heat.

Spread 1 1/2 teaspoons olive oil in a 9×13-inch baking pan. Drain the noodles and arrange five noodles in the prepared pan. Layer half the cottage cheese, half the spinach, one-third of the Monterey Jack cheese and half the vegetable mixture over the noodles. Repeat the layers and top with the remaining Monterey Jack cheese. Sprinkle with the Parmesan cheese. Bake at 375 degrees for 45 minutes.

SERVES 12

Vegetables & Side Dishes

Political Appetite

Arkansas State Capitol

The Arkansas State Capitol, located at the end of West Capitol Avenue, is the seat of state government in Arkansas and the cornerstone of the Capitol Mall area. Construction on the building took sixteen years to complete, from 1899 to 1915. With the cupola covered in twenty-four-karat gold leaf, the exterior of the Capitol is made of limestone that was quarried in Batesville, Arkansas. The front entrance doors are made of bronze and were purchased from Tiffany's in New York. The State Capitol was modeled after the United States Capitol in Washington, D.C., and stands as one of our nation's most elegant structures. Take a tour of the Capitol and get a taste of our state's laws, legends, and legacies.

Baked Acorn Squash with Sausage Stuffing

SAUSAGE STUFFING

16 ounces Italian sausage, casings removed and sausage crumbled
2   tablespoons olive oil
1   onion, finely chopped
1/2 green bell pepper, finely chopped
1   tablespoon minced garlic
1/2 cup chicken stock
4   cups cubed French bread
1/2 cup (2 ounces) shredded mozzarella cheese
1/2 cup (2 ounces) shredded Monterey Jack cheese
1   tablespoon finely chopped Italian flat-leaf parsley

1   teaspoon dried sage
1   egg
    Salt and freshly ground pepper to taste

ACORN SQUASH

4   acorn squash
1   tablespoon olive oil
    Salt and freshly ground pepper to taste
1/2 cup water
1/2 cup (2 ounces) shredded mozzarella cheese
1/2 cup (2 ounces) shredded Monterey Jack cheese

Brown the sausage in a large skillet, stirring until crumbly; remove to a bowl and drain the skillet. Heat the olive oil in the skillet and add the onion and green bell pepper. Sauté until tender. Add the garlic and sauté for 1 minute.

Add to the sausage in the bowl and stir in the chicken stock, bread cubes, mozzarella cheese, Monterey Jack cheese, parsley and sage. Add the egg and mix well. Season with salt and pepper.

Cut the squash into halves and discard the seeds. Brush the cut sides with the olive oil and season with salt and pepper. Place cut side down in a baking pan and add the water. Cover lightly with foil and bake at 350 degrees for 1 hour or until tender. Cool completely.

Spoon the stuffing into the squash halves and top with the mozzarella cheese and Monterey Jack cheese. Place on a baking sheet and bake for 25 minutes or until heated through.

SERVES 8

Asparagus Dijon

1 cup mayonnaise
1/2 cup Dijon mustard
    Juice of 1 lemon
1 pound fresh asparagus

1¹/2 cups panko bread crumbs
3/4 cup (3 ounces) grated
    Parmesan cheese

Combine the mayonnaise, Dijon mustard and lemon juice in a shallow dish. Trim the tough ends of the asparagus spears. Add the asparagus to the Dijon mustard mixture and turn to coat well. Chill in the refrigerator.

Mix the bread crumbs and cheese in a shallow dish. Remove the asparagus from the sauce; reserve the sauce. Add the asparagus to the crumb mixture and turn to coat evenly.

Arrange on a baking sheet lined with foil. Bake at 375 degrees for 12 to 15 minutes or until tender. Serve with the reserved sauce.

SERVES 4

Marinated Asparagus

1/2 cup extra-virgin olive oil
1/4 cup balsamic vinegar
2 tablespoons grainy mustard
3 garlic cloves, minced
    Pinch of sugar

2 or 3 basil leaves, crushed
1 sprig of rosemary
    Salt and pepper to taste
1 bunch fresh asparagus

Whisk the olive oil, vinegar, mustard, garlic, sugar, basil, rosemary, salt and pepper in a bowl until combined.

Blanch the asparagus briefly in boiling water in a saucepan; drain and place in ice water to cool. Combine with the marinade in a sealable plastic bag; seal and turn to coat well. Marinate in the refrigerator for 20 minutes to 12 hours.

SERVES 4

Asparagus Soufflés

Béchamel Sauce

3 tablespoons butter
3 tablespoons all-purpose flour
1 1/4 cups milk
1/8 teaspoon dry mustard
1/8 teaspoon ground cumin
1/8 teaspoon ground ginger
    Freshly ground pepper to taste

Asparagus

1 pound fresh asparagus
1 teaspoon salt

1/4 cup chopped shallots
1 garlic clove, chopped
1 teaspoon chopped fresh thyme
1 tablespoon butter
3 egg yolks, lightly beaten
5 egg whites
    Pinch of salt
1/2 cup (2 ounces) grated
    Gruyère cheese
1/2 cup seasoned dry bread crumbs

Melt the butter in a saucepan and whisk in the flour. Cook for several minutes, stirring constantly. Add the milk gradually and cook until smooth, stirring constantly. Stir in the dry mustard, cumin, ginger and pepper. Reduce the heat and simmer for 15 minutes, stirring occasionally.

Trim the tough ends of the asparagus and cut the spears into 1-inch pieces. Add 1 teaspoon salt to a saucepan of boiling water. Add the asparagus and blanch briefly; drain and place in ice water to cool.

Sauté the shallots, garlic and thyme in the butter in a saucepan over medium heat for 5 minutes. Combine with the asparagus in a food processor and process until puréed.

Combine the purée with the béchamel sauce in a large bowl. Add the egg yolks and mix well. Combine the egg whites with a pinch of salt in a mixing bowl and beat until soft peaks form. Fold gradually into the asparagus mixture. Fold in the cheese.

Sprinkle the bread crumbs into six buttered 8-ounce ramekins and shake to coat well. Shake out and reserve the excess crumbs. Spoon the asparagus mixture into the prepared ramekins, filling to within 1/4 inch of the top. Sprinkle with the reserved bread crumbs.

Place the ramekins in a 9×12-inch baking pan. Add enough boiling water to the baking pan to reach halfway up the sides of the ramekins. Bake at 400 degrees for 10 minutes. Reduce the oven temperature to 350 degrees and bake for 15 minutes longer. Do not open the oven during the baking time to prevent the soufflés from falling.

Serves 6

Prosciutto-Wrapped Asparagus

1   bunch asparagus, trimmed
4   ounces thinly sliced prosciutto, cut
    into halves
    Juice of 1 lemon
    Extra-virgin olive oil
1/2 teaspoon Greek seasoning
    (tested with Cavender's Seasoning)
1/2 cup (2 ounces) grated asiago cheese

Place the asparagus in the rack of a steamer pot. Steam over boiling water for 3 to 4 minutes. Arrange the asparagus in bundles of three or four spears. Wrap one-half slice of prosciutto around each bundle.

Arrange the bundles seam side down in a 9×13-inch baking dish. Drizzle with the lemon juice and olive oil. Sprinkle with the Greek seasoning and cheese. Bake at 350 degrees for 15 minutes or until the cheese melts.

SERVES 4 TO 6

Arkansas Women in Government

Without question, women have played a significant role in the political and governmental arenas of Arkansas. A review of our history demonstrates the key roles they have played in federal, state, county, and municipal responsibilities. In 1932 Hattie Wyatt Caraway of Arkansas became the first woman ever elected to the United States Senate. She was also the first woman to chair a Senate committee and the first woman to preside formally over the Senate as acting president pro tempore. In 1998 Blanche Lambert Lincoln of Arkansas—at age 38—became the youngest woman elected to the U.S. Senate and is serving as Democratic Caucus Chair for Rural Outreach. Lottie Shackleford became the first woman elected Mayor of Little Rock in 1987 and has since become the longest-serving vice chair of the National Democratic Party in American history. As the movie serials used to say: "To Be Continued."

Riverfront Fireworks Watch Party

Black-Eyed Pea Dip

22

Summer Greens and Berries

56

Warm Steak and Potato Salad

64

Green Bean Sauté

133

Off-the-Cob Creamed Corn

140

Strawberry Layer Cake

207

Wine: Sauvignon Blanc and Pinot Noir

Five-Bean Bake

8	slices bacon	1	(14-ounce) can butter beans, drained
1	large onion, chopped		
1	cup packed brown sugar	1	(14-ounce) can lima beans, drained
1/2	cup vinegar		
1	teaspoon dry mustard	1	(14-ounce) can pinto beans, drained
1/2	teaspoon garlic powder		
1/2	teaspoon salt	1	(28-ounce) can baked beans
1	(14-ounce) can cut green beans, drained		

Cook the bacon in a skillet until crisp. Drain on paper towels and crumble. Add the onion to the drippings in the skillet and sauté until tender. Stir in the brown sugar, vinegar, dry mustard, garlic powder and salt. Cook until the brown sugar melts, stirring to mix well.

Combine the green beans, butter beans, lima beans, pinto beans and baked beans in a bowl. Add the sauce mixture and bacon and mix well. Spoon into a baking dish. Bake at 350 degrees for 45 minutes.

SERVES 10

Green Bean Sauté

12	ounces fresh green beans, trimmed	1	garlic clove, minced
			Kosher salt and freshly ground pepper to taste
1 1/2	tablespoons butter		
1	shallot, minced		Grated zest of 1 lemon
1/2	cup grape tomato halves	2	teaspoons lemon juice

Place the green beans in a microwave-safe container. Microwave, covered with plastic wrap, on High for 3 minutes or until tender-crisp.

Melt the butter in a skillet over medium-high heat. Add the shallot and sauté for 3 minutes or until tender. Add the green beans, tomatoes, garlic, kosher salt and pepper; mix well. Sauté for 2 minutes. Remove from the heat and add the lemon zest and lemon juice; toss to coat evenly.

SERVES 4

Mediterranean Green Beans

1	pound fresh green beans, trimmed	1/4	cup red wine vinegar
2	tablespoons olive oil	1	tablespoon dried oregano
1	small onion, thinly sliced into rings	6	tablespoons crumbled feta cheese
2	garlic cloves, minced		Kalamata olives (optional)
2	tomatoes, chopped, or 1 (16-ounce) can tomatoes		Pepper to taste

Add the beans to a saucepan of boiling water. Reduce the heat and simmer for 4 minutes. Drain the beans and place in cold water to refresh.

Heat the olive oil in a large skillet. Add the onion and garlic and sauté until tender. Add the tomatoes, vinegar and oregano. Simmer for 5 minutes, stirring frequently. Drain the beans and add to the skillet. Simmer until heated through. Spoon into a serving bowl and sprinkle with the cheese, olives and pepper.

SERVES 4

Pesto Green Beans

1	cup loosely packed basil leaves	1/2	teaspoon salt
2	tablespoons walnuts	1/4	teaspoon pepper
1	garlic clove	1	pound fresh green beans, trimmed
1/4	cup olive oil		

Combine the basil, walnuts and garlic in a food processor. Process until finely chopped, scraping down the side of the processor as needed. Add the olive oil gradually, processing constantly until smooth. Season with the salt and pepper.

Place the green beans in the rack of a steamer pot and steam over boiling water for 6 to 8 minutes or until tender-crisp. Drain and toss with the pesto mixture.

SERVES 4

Broccoli with Lemon Crumbs

$^1/_2$ cup homemade bread crumbs
$^1/_4$ cup ($^1/_2$ stick) butter
1   tablespoon grated lemon zest
3   tablespoons butter
1   garlic clove, minced
$^1/_2$ teaspoon salt
    Coarsely ground pepper to taste
1$^1/_2$ pounds broccoli, cooked and drained

Sauté the bread crumbs in $^1/_4$ cup butter in a large skillet until light brown. Remove to a bowl with a slotted spoon and add the lemon zest; mix well.

Melt 3 tablespoons butter in the skillet and add the garlic, salt and pepper. Cook until the butter is light brown. Add the broccoli and turn to coat well. Spoon the broccoli into a serving dish and top with the lemon crumbs.

SERVES 6

Arkansas Governor's Mansion

*Located on Center Street in the historic Quapaw Quarter District, the
Arkansas Governor's Mansion has been the official residence of our state's chief executive
since 1950. The Georgian Colonial mansion is flanked by two colonnaded
walkways that link the mansion to two cottages. Through the colonnades, visitors can view the
gardens that frame the home. The eight and one-half acres feature one of the
largest herb gardens maintained by the National Herb Society, as well as a vegetable garden,
which is an ongoing project of the Arkansas Master Gardeners. With a multi-million
dollar renovation and expansion from 2000 through 2002, the mansion is a charming home
to welcome and entertain dignitaries from around the globe. Call the mansion
to schedule an individual tour and experience its grandeur for yourself!*

Brussels Sprouts with Pine Nuts

6   *slices bacon*
1/4 *cup pine nuts*
1/3 *cup chopped onion*
1   *pound brussels sprouts, cut into halves*
     Juice of 1 lemon

Cook the bacon in a large skillet until crisp. Drain on paper towels and crumble. Drain all but 1 tablespoon of the drippings from the skillet. Add the pine nuts to the skillet and sauté until golden brown. Add the onion and sauté until translucent.

Add the brussels sprouts and stir-fry for 3 minutes or until tender-crisp and just beginning to wilt. Combine with the lemon juice and crumbled bacon in a bowl and mix well. Serve with roasted chicken and baked sweet potatoes for a good fall menu.

SERVES 4 TO 6

Chef to the Governors

The Arkansan with the longest tenure in the Govenor's Mansion was not a Clinton or a Faubus, but a chocolate-chip cookie aficionada named Liza Ashley. She was hired in the 1950s as the mansion cook by Alta Faubus because the First Lady preferred to have a woman do the cooking. Liza prepared meals for governors whose favorites ranged from duck breasts to turnip greens. Always flexible and with a flavorful flair, she prepared every type of meal, from dinners for presidents to special infant treats. Liza's special brand of Southern cooking secured her place in Arkansas's culinary history.

Balsamic-Glazed Cabbage

4	slices bacon, chopped	1/4	teaspoon kosher salt
1	head cabbage, cored and cut into 2-inch pieces	1/8	teaspoon freshly ground pepper
		1	tablespoon brown sugar
1	tablespoon water	2	tablespoons balsamic vinegar

Cook the bacon in a large saucepan over medium-high heat for 2 to 3 minutes or until brown. Add the cabbage, water, kosher salt and pepper. Cook, covered, for 4 to 5 minutes or until the cabbage begins to wilt, stirring once if needed. Cook for 5 to 10 minutes longer or until the cabbage is done to taste and slightly caramelized on the edges.

Whisk the brown sugar and balsamic vinegar in a small bowl. Add to the cabbage and toss to coat well. Serve immediately. This is a wonderful accompaniment for pork.

SERVES 4 TO 6

Candied Carrots

1	bunch young organic carrots with tops		Juice and grated zest of 1 orange
1/4	cup olive oil	2	tablespoons brown sugar
	Salt and pepper to taste	1	tablespoon granulated sugar
1/4	cup (1/2 stick) butter	1	teaspoon cinnamon
	Juice of 1 lemon	1	teaspoon ground cumin
		1/4	teaspoon nutmeg

Slice off the tops of the carrots, leaving 1 inch of the stems. Place in a 9×13-inch baking dish and drizzle with the olive oil; sprinkle with salt and pepper. Roast at 350 degrees for 30 minutes or until fork-tender.

Melt the butter in a skillet over medium-low heat. Add the lemon juice, orange juice, orange zest, brown sugar, granulated sugar, cinnamon, cumin and nutmeg; mix well. Cook for 2 minutes or until syrupy. Drizzle over the carrots in a serving bowl.

SERVES 4

Lemon Basil Carrots

1	pound baby carrots	1/2	teaspoon lemon juice
1	tablespoon butter	1/2	teaspoon garlic salt
1	tablespoon chopped fresh basil		Pepper to taste

Place the carrots in the rack of a steamer pot and steam over boiling water for 10 to 15 minutes or until tender.

Combine the butter, basil, lemon juice, garlic salt and pepper in a saucepan. Cook over low heat until the butter melts, stirring to mix well. Add the carrots and mix gently.

SERVES 8

Cauliflower Gratin

1	head cauliflower	2	cups (8 ounces) shredded
1/4	teaspoon salt		Cheddar cheese
1/4	teaspoon pepper	1	tablespoon sesame seeds, roasted
1	cup sour cream		

Remove the large outer leaves of the cauliflower and break the cauliflower into florets. Season a small amount of water with the salt and pepper in a large saucepan and bring to a boil. Add the cauliflower and cook, covered, for 8 to 10 minutes or until tender; drain.

Layer the cauliflower, sour cream, cheese and sesame seeds one-half at a time in a 1-quart baking dish. Bake at 350 degrees for 10 to 15 minutes or until heated through.

SERVES 4 TO 6

At Home in the Mansion

"It was not long after moving into the Governor's Mansion that our family began to call Little Rock home. Little Rock was more than we had hoped for; it was culturally enriching and stimulating. Our children quickly adjusted to life in Little Rock. After leaving the mansion, we continue to call Little Rock home even if we are housed elsewhere."

—United States Senator and Mrs. Dale Bumpers
Arkansas Governor 1971–1975

Off-the-Cob Creamed Corn

10   ears fresh corn, husks and silk removed, or
     2 (16-ounce) packages frozen corn kernels
1   cup heavy cream
1   cup milk
2   tablespoons sugar
1/2 teaspoon thyme
1   teaspoon kosher salt
1/2 teaspoon white pepper
1/2 teaspoon black pepper
1/2 cup (1 stick) butter
1   garlic clove, minced
1   scallion, chopped
1   jalapeño chile, seeded and minced
1   tablespoon all-purpose flour

Cook the corn in enough water to cover in a large saucepan until tender; drain and cool slightly. Cut the kernels from the ears with a sharp knife. Combine the corn kernels with the cream, milk, sugar, thyme, kosher salt, white pepper and black pepper in a large stockpot. Bring gradually to a boil. Reduce the heat and simmer for 3 minutes.

Heat the butter in a saucepan until bubbly. Add the garlic, scallion and jalapeño chile and sauté until tender. Stir in the flour until smooth. Add to the corn mixture and simmer for 3 minutes, stirring occasionally. Serve immediately or keep warm until serving time.

SERVES 8

Corn off the Cob

Cutting corn from the cob is much easier when using a bundt pan with a hole in the center. Holding the bottom or stem end of a husked ear of corn, place the top or pointed end of the ear into the hole to provide stability and allow it to stand upright. Carefully run a knife down the side of the corn until you have removed all the kernels. The kernels will fall into the well of the bundt pan for easy collection and cleanup.

Parmesan Eggplant Sticks

1	eggplant	1	garlic clove, minced
1/2	cup (2 ounces) grated Parmesan cheese		Salt and pepper to taste
1/4	cup seasoned bread crumbs	1/4	cup all-purpose flour
1	tablespoon chopped parsley	1	egg, beaten
		1	tablespoon butter

*P*eel the eggplant and cut into sticks. Combine the cheese, bread crumbs, parsley, garlic, salt and pepper in a shallow dish. Dust the eggplant with the flour and dip into the egg. Coat with the bread crumb mixture.

Melt the butter in a baking pan and arrange the eggplant in the pan. Bake at 400 degrees for 25 minutes.

SERVES 4

Braised Fennel

1	large fennel bulb with green top		Salt and pepper to taste
2 to 3 cups chicken stock		1/2	cup heavy cream
	Butter to taste		Grated Parmesan cheese to taste

*R*emove the green top from the fennel bulb and reserve. Cut the fennel bulb into quarters or smaller pieces. Combine with just enough chicken stock to cover in a saucepan. Season with butter, salt and pepper. Cook, covered, until the fennel can be pierced easily with a knife; drain, reserving the cooking liquid. Place the fennel in a small au gratin dish.

Add the cream to the reserved cooking liquid in the saucepan. Bring to a boil and cook until reduced to the desired consistency. Pour over the fennel and sprinkle with cheese. Bake at 400 degrees until brown on top. Garnish with some of the chopped reserved fennel top.

SERVES 4

Grilled Stuffed Portobello Mushrooms

4	portobello mushrooms
1/4	cup olive oil
2	tablespoons lemon juice
2	teaspoons soy sauce
1 1/2	cups panko bread crumbs
1	cup (4 ounces) shredded Monterey Jack cheese
3/4	cup seeded chopped plum tomatoes
1/4	cup chopped green onions
2	garlic cloves, minced
2	tablespoons olive oil
1	tablespoon chopped fresh oregano
2	teaspoons chopped fresh thyme
1	teaspoon chopped fresh rosemary
	Salt and pepper to taste
1/4	cup (1 ounce) shredded Monterey Jack cheese

Discard the stems and scoop out the gills of the mushrooms with a spoon. Combine 1/4 cup olive oil with the lemon juice and soy sauce in a small bowl and whisk until smooth. Brush over both sides of the mushroom caps and arrange gill side up on a baking sheet. Let stand at room temperature for 30 minutes.

Combine the bread crumbs, 1 cup cheese, the tomatoes, green onions, garlic, 2 tablespoons olive oil, the oregano, thyme, rosemary, salt and pepper in a bowl; mix well. Spoon onto the mushrooms, leaving a 1/2-inch border around the edge of each mushroom and pressing down lightly. Sprinkle with 1/4 cup cheese.

Place stuffing side up on a grill heated to medium. Close the grill and grill for 6 minutes or until the cheese melts and the mushrooms are bubbly at the edges. Rearrange on the grill if necessary for even cooking; do not overcook.

SERVES 8

Sugar Snap Peas with Cashews

2   tablespoons vegetable oil
1   pound sugar snap peas
2   garlic cloves, minced
1   tablespoon mirin
1   teaspoon soy sauce
1   cup cashews
1   tablespoon hoisin sauce
1/2   teaspoon chili garlic sauce

Heat the oil in a wok or large skillet. Add the peas and stir-fry for 3 minutes. Add the garlic and stir-fry for 1 minute. Stir in the mirin and soy sauce and cook for several minutes or until the liquid has been absorbed.

Add the cashews, hoisin sauce and chili garlic sauce. Cook for 1 to 2 minutes or until the mixture is heated through and the flavors blend.

SERVES 8

Southern Cooking Asian-Style

"One of the things you learn when you grow up in the South is how important food is to special occasions. That similarity with Chinese and Japanese culture is one of the things that attracted me to the cuisine of Southeast Asia. There is a great deal of care and attention that goes into the preparation of each dish, with all the chopping and dicing of ingredients and the focus on color and freshness. We hand-make our Chinese spring rolls with the same care and love that my grandmother showed when she cracked and shelled the pecans for our pecan pies. Learning about food as it relates to the culture of China and Japan has greatly increased my appreciation of what both my grandmothers and my mother did in their kitchens."

—Kathy Webb
Executive Chef/Co-owner, Lilly's Dim Sum, Then Some

Caramelized Onion and White Cheddar Potatoes

12	red potatoes, peeled and thinly sliced
1	teaspoon salt
2	tablespoons butter
2	tablespoons olive oil
1	large onion, chopped
4	garlic cloves, minced
1/2	teaspoon white pepper
2	teaspoons chopped fresh rosemary
1/4	cup (1/2 stick) butter
1/3	cup all-purpose flour
2 1/2	cups half-and-half
1	cup dry white wine
1/4	teaspoon salt
2	cups (8 ounces) shredded white Cheddar cheese
1	teaspoon salt

Combine the potatoes with 1 teaspoon salt and enough water to cover in a large saucepan or Dutch oven. Bring to a boil and cook for 8 to 10 minutes or until tender; drain.

Melt 2 tablespoons butter with the olive oil in a skillet over medium heat. Add the onion, garlic and white pepper. Sauté for 15 minutes or until golden brown. Stir in the rosemary and remove from the heat.

Melt 1/4 cup butter in a saucepan over low heat. Whisk in the flour. Cook for 1 minute, whisking constantly. Whisk in the half-and-half and wine. Cook over medium heat for 20 minutes or until thickened and bubbly, whisking constantly. Stir in 1/4 teaspoon salt.

Layer the potatoes, onion mixture, cheese and cream sauce one-half at a time in a lightly greased 9×13-inch baking dish, sprinkling each layer of potatoes with 1/2 teaspoon salt. Bake at 350 degrees for 1 hour or until golden brown.

SERVES 10

Mashed Garlic New Potatoes

5	pounds new potatoes	1/2	cup (1 stick) butter, softened
1/2	cup heavy whipping cream, whipped	1	garlic clove, minced
3	tablespoons sour cream		Salt and pepper to taste
			Chopped parsley, for garnish

*C*ut the unpeeled potatoes into small pieces and combine with enough water to cover in a saucepan. Cook until very tender. Drain and mash the potatoes in the saucepan. Add the whipped cream, sour cream, butter, garlic, salt and pepper and mix well. Spoon into a serving dish. Serve immediately or store in the refrigerator and reheat at 350 degrees to serve later. Garnish with parsley.

SERVES 10 TO 12

Smoky Cheddar Potato Bake

8	potatoes, peeled and cut into cubes	1/4	cup (1 ounce) grated Parmesan cheese
6	slices applewood-smoked bacon, chopped		Leaves of 4 sprigs of fresh thyme
2	shallots, chopped		Sea salt and freshly ground pepper to taste
1	cup heavy cream	1	cup (4 ounces) shredded smoked Cheddar cheese
3	tablespoons chopped chives		Chopped chives, for garnish
1/2	cup (2 ounces) shredded smoked Cheddar cheese		

*P*lace the potatoes in a saucepan and add enough water to cover. Boil until the potatoes are fork-tender; drain and place in a mixing bowl.

Cook the bacon in a skillet over medium-high heat until crisp. Add the shallots and sauté until translucent. Remove the bacon and shallots with a slotted spoon; set aside.

Add the cream to the potatoes and beat until smooth. Add the bacon mixture, 3 tablespoons chives, 1/2 cup Cheddar cheese, the Parmesan cheese, thyme, sea salt and pepper; mix well. Spoon into a 2-quart baking dish and sprinkle with 1 cup Cheddar cheese. Bake at 350 degrees for 15 to 20 minutes or until the cheese melts. Garnish with additional chives.

SERVES 8

Herbed Fingerling Potatoes

2	pounds red or yellow fingerling potatoes or small new potatoes
4	cups chicken broth
	Kosher salt to taste
1/4	cup dry vermouth
	Freshly ground pepper to taste
1/3	cup extra-virgin olive oil
1	shallot, minced
1	garlic clove, minced
1/4	cup lemon juice
1	teaspoon Dijon mustard
1	tablespoon minced fresh basil leaves
1 1/2	teaspoons minced fresh thyme

Cut the unpeeled potatoes into halves. Combine with the chicken broth in a large saucepan and season with kosher salt. Add enough cold water to cover the potatoes by 1 inch. Bring to a boil and reduce the heat. Simmer for 6 to 8 minutes or until fork-tender; drain.

Combine the potatoes with the vermouth in a large bowl and season with kosher salt and pepper; toss to coat well. Let stand, covered, for 1 minute or longer.

Heat the olive oil in a skillet over medium-high heat. Add the shallot and sauté for 2 minutes. Add the garlic and sauté for 1 minute longer. Reduce the heat to low and whisk in the lemon juice, Dijon mustard, basil and thyme. Season with kosher salt and pepper. Pour over the potatoes and toss to mix well. Serve warm or at room temperature.

SERVES 6 TO 8

A Historical Mansion

"Nothing in the state can match Little Rock for its history. One of my most satisfying experiences as a writer and historian has been a private tour through the 4,000-square-foot mansion at Fourteenth and Scott. Built in 1873 by Redeemer Governor Augustus Garland, the house was later rented during the First World War to Governor Charles Hillman Brough and his suffragette wife, Anne, by William Starr Mitchell, whose wife's father had been a wealthy carpetbagger. After dinner, Arkansas's most educated governor ever could usually be found upstairs in the library with his six thousand books."

—Griffin Stockley
Author

Spinach Couscous Casserole

1¹/2 cups chicken stock
1   cup uncooked couscous
¹/2 teaspoon salt
¹/4 cup olive oil
1   large onion, chopped
3   large garlic cloves, minced
1   (28-ounce) can plum tomatoes (tested with
      San Marzano-style tomatoes)
6   ounces fresh spinach, coarsely chopped (about 5 cups)
1¹/2 tablespoons chopped fresh basil
      Freshly ground pepper to taste
1   cup (4 ounces) shredded Monterey Jack cheese
¹/3 cup pine nuts

Bring the chicken stock to a boil in a saucepan. Combine with the couscous and salt in a bowl. Cover with a plate and let stand for 5 minutes. Fluff with a fork.

Heat the olive oil in a large skillet. Add the onion and garlic and sauté until the onion is tender and translucent. Drain the tomatoes, reserving 1/3 cup juice. Chop the tomatoes and add to the skillet. Remove from the heat.

Add the reserved tomato juice, couscous, spinach, basil and pepper; mix well. Spread half the couscous mixture in a 2-quart or 7×12-inch baking dish. Sprinkle with the cheese and spread with the remaining couscous mixture. Top with the pine nuts. Cover with foil and bake at 375 degrees for 25 minutes. You can also prepare the dish and store it in the refrigerator to bake later.

SERVES 6 TO 8

Spinach Ring with Tomatoes

^{1}/2   cup chopped onion
^{1}/4   cup (^{1}/2 stick) butter
2   (10-ounce) packages frozen chopped spinach
^{3}/4   cup light cream
4   eggs, lightly beaten
^{3}/4   cup milk
^{1}/4   teaspoon garlic salt
1   teaspoon salt
2   tablespoons grated Parmesan cheese
2   tablespoons butter
1   pint cherry tomatoes or grape tomatoes
2   teaspoons finely chopped fresh oregano
^{1}/2   teaspoon salt

Sauté the onion in ^{1}/4 cup butter in a saucepan. Add the spinach. Cook, covered, for 5 minutes or until completely thawed, stirring occasionally to separate. Remove the cover and cook until the liquid has evaporated, stirring occasionally. Stir in the cream and simmer for 2 minutes.

Beat the eggs with the milk, garlic salt and 1 teaspoon salt in a medium bowl. Stir in the spinach mixture and cheese. Spoon into a buttered 5^1/2-cup ring mold and place in a shallow baking pan. Add 1 inch hot water to the pan. Cover the mold with waxed paper. Bake at 325 degrees for 40 minutes or until a knife inserted near the center comes out clean.

Heat 2 tablespoons butter in a medium skillet and stir in the tomatoes, oregano and ^{1}/2 teaspoon salt. Cook over medium heat for 3 to 5 minutes; keep warm.

Loosen the spinach ring from the side and center of the mold with a small spatula. Invert onto a heated plate and spoon the tomatoes into the center.

SERVES 8

Pancetta Spinach Cups

1   (10-ounce) package frozen spinach, thawed
1   tablespoon olive oil
1/2   cup finely chopped onion
3   garlic cloves, minced
3   eggs
3/4   cup heavy cream
1/4   teaspoon salt
1/2   teaspoon freshly ground black pepper
     Cayenne pepper to taste
     Nutmeg to taste
1/4   cup chopped cooked pancetta
1 1/2 cups (6 ounces) grated Parmesan cheese

Press the spinach to remove excess moisture. Heat the olive oil in a skillet over medium-high heat. Add the spinach, onion and garlic to the skillet and sauté for 4 minutes or until the moisture evaporates, stirring constantly. Pour into a fine mesh strainer and press to remove the moisture.

Combine the spinach with the eggs, cream, salt, black pepper, cayenne pepper and nutmeg in a food processor. Pulse until the spinach is finely chopped. Combine the spinach mixture with the pancetta and cheese in a bowl; mix well.

Spoon into four 6-ounce ramekins brushed with olive oil. Bake at 400 degrees for 20 minutes or until set around the edges and soft in the centers. Turn off the oven and let the ramekins stand in the closed oven for 5 minutes longer. Loosen from the edges of the ramekins with a knife and invert onto serving plates. Serve warm.

SERVES 4

149

Vegetables & Side Dishes

The Old State House

One of the most impressive examples of antebellum architecture in the South, The Old State House on Markham Avenue is the oldest surviving state capitol building west of the Mississippi. The building was the official seat of state government from 1836 — the year Arkansas gained statehood—until 1911, when the current capitol opened. Millions around the world were exposed to this landmark when then-Governor Bill Clinton announced his presidential bid at its entrance in 1991 and then celebrated his 1992 and 1996 presidential victories on its front steps. Make your own history by exploring its halls and archives during your visit to Little Rock.

Chipotle Sweet Potato Casserole

PECAN TOPPING

1	cup packed brown sugar
1/3	cup all-purpose flour
1/2	cup chopped pecans
1	teaspoon salt
2	teaspoons crushed red pepper flakes
1/2	teaspoon cayenne pepper
2	tablespoons butter

SWEET POTATOES

4	large sweet potatoes
	Olive oil for rubbing
1 1/2	cups heavy cream
1 to 2	tablespoons puréed chipotle chiles in adobo sauce
1/2	cup (1 stick) unsalted butter, softened
1/2	cup molasses
1/4	cup crème fraîche
	Salt and freshly ground pepper to taste

Combine the brown sugar, flour, pecans, salt, red pepper and cayenne pepper in a bowl. Cut in the butter with a pastry knife or fork until crumbly.

Rub the sweet potatoes lightly with olive oil and place on a baking sheet. Bake at 375 degrees for 45 to 50 minutes or until tender. Remove from the oven and let stand for 5 minutes. Cut into halves lengthwise and scoop into a bowl, discarding the skins.

Combine the cream with the chipotle chiles in a saucepan and bring to a simmer over low heat. Add to the sweet potatoes with the butter, molasses and crème fraîche; mix until smooth. Season with salt and pepper. Spread in a greased 9×13-inch baking dish. Sprinkle with the pecan topping. Bake at 350 degrees for 45 minutes.

SERVES 10

A Town with a Future

"In Little Rock, I experienced many things that prepared me for life. Today, as I share my time between Arkansas and Washington, D.C., I get to see Little Rock from a different perspective. The city and area have changed a lot since I was a child, but the change has been positive. Of all the assets Little Rock offers, there is one intangible that still makes it a wonderful place to live—people in the community are dedicated to making our future even better."

—Mark Pryor
United States Senator

Harvest Supper

Autumn Salad

59

Pork Tenderloin

87

Brussels Sprouts with Pine Nuts

136

Chipotle Sweet Potato Casserole

150

White Chocolate Bread Pudding

236

Wine: German Riesling

Rivermarket Squash Cakes

2	yellow squash, grated	1	egg, beaten
1	zucchini, grated	3/4	cup self-rising white cornmeal
1	Vidalia onion, grated	3/4	cup self-rising flour
1	cup finely chopped red		Salt and pepper to taste
	bell pepper		Vegetable oil for sautéing
2	tablespoons chopped fresh chives		

*M*ix the yellow squash, zucchini, onion, red bell pepper and chives in a large bowl. Add the egg, cornmeal, flour, salt and pepper and mix well. Shape into small cakes.

Heat about 1 inch of oil in a large skillet over high heat. Add the squash cakes and sauté for 5 to 7 minutes on each side or until golden brown. Drain on paper towels. Serve hot. You can vary the dish by adding corn, cheese or herbs to the mixture and serving with aïoli or rémoulade, if desired.

SERVES 8

Sweet Potato Fries with Maple Sauce

SWEET POTATO FRIES		MAPLE DIPPING SAUCE	
6	sweet potatoes	1/2	cup maple syrup
1/4	cup olive oil	2	tablespoons plain yogurt
2	tablespoons chopped fresh basil	1	teaspoon cinnamon
1	tablespoon kosher salt	1/2	teaspoon nutmeg
1/2	teaspoon freshly ground pepper		Cayenne pepper to taste

*S*lice the sweet potatoes into sticks 1/2 inch wide. Drizzle with the olive oil on a baking sheet and toss to coat well. Arrange in a single layer. Bake at 400 degrees for 40 minutes or until cooked through. Combine the basil, kosher salt and pepper in a bowl. Sprinkle over the sweet potatoes.

*C*ombine the maple syrup, yogurt, cinnamon, nutmeg and cayenne pepper in a jar with a tight-fitting lid and seal tightly. Shake to mix well. Serve with the fries.

SERVES 6

Tomato Pie

3 to 5 tomatoes
   Salt to taste
1   small onion, chopped
1   unbaked (9-inch) pie shell
1   tablespoon lemon juice

3 to 4 tablespoons chopped fresh basil
   Pepper to taste
1   cup mayonnaise
1¹/₂ cups (6 ounces) shredded sharp
   Cheddar cheese

*S*lice the tomatoes and sprinkle with salt. Let stand to drain for 20 minutes; pat dry with paper towels. Sprinkle the onion in the pie shell. Layer the tomatoes over the onion. Drizzle with the lemon juice and sprinkle with the basil, salt and pepper.

Combine the mayonnaise and cheese in a bowl and mix well. Spread over the tomatoes. Bake at 350 degrees for 30 to 45 minutes or until brown on top. Cut into wedges to serve.

SERVES 8

Tomatoes Rockefeller

5   large tomatoes
   Salt to taste
2   (10-ounce) packages frozen
   chopped spinach, thawed
1   bunch green onions
1   bunch parsley

1   rib celery
1   cup (2 sticks) butter, melted
¹/₂ cup toasted bread crumbs
2   tablespoons Worcestershire sauce
   Tarragon to taste
   Freshly ground pepper to taste

*C*ut the tomatoes into twelve thick slices and sprinkle with salt. Let stand to drain for 20 minutes. Pat dry and arrange on a baking sheet.

Cook the spinach using the package directions. Drain and press to remove the excess moisture. Combine the spinach, green onions, parsley and celery in a food processor and process until finely chopped. Add the butter, bread crumbs, Worcestershire sauce, tarragon, salt and pepper and mix well.

Mound the spinach mixture on the tomato slices. Bake at 350 degrees for 12 to 15 minutes or until heated through.

SERVES 12

Grilled Vegetables

6	tablespoons olive oil	3	zucchini, thickly sliced
2	tablespoons balsamic vinegar	1	red onion, thickly sliced
1	teaspoon oregano	2	portobello mushroom caps,
	Salt and pepper to taste		thickly sliced
3	Japanese eggplant, thickly sliced		Olive oil for brushing
2	red bell peppers, thickly sliced		Crumbled goat cheese to taste
1	yellow bell pepper, thickly sliced		

Combine 6 tablespoons olive oil, the vinegar, oregano, salt and pepper in a bowl for the vinaigrette.

Brush the eggplant, red bell peppers, yellow bell pepper, zucchini, onion and mushrooms with additional olive oil. Grill the vegetables until tender. Cut into strips and add to the vinaigrette mixture. Sprinkle with goat cheese.

SERVES 4

Spring Vegetables with Crisp Shallots

4	ounces French green beans (haricots verts), trimmed	4	ounces asparagus, trimmed and cut into 2-inch pieces
	Salt to taste	2	tablespoons butter
4	ounces sugar snap peas	1	tablespoon olive oil
8	ounces broccolini, trimmed and cut into halves	3	large shallots, sliced
		1	teaspoon freshly ground pepper

Add the green beans to a large saucepan of boiling salted water. Blanch for 1 minute. Remove to a large bowl of ice water with a slotted spoon. Repeat the process with the sugar snap peas and broccolini. Blanch the asparagus for 2 minutes and place in the ice water. Drain the vegetables well.

Heat the butter with the olive oil in a large skillet. Add the shallots and sauté for 5 minutes or until light brown. Add the drained vegetables and sauté until heated through. Season with salt and pepper and toss to mix well.

SERVES 6

Forest Floor Tart

1	refrigerator pie pastry, at room temperature		3	eggs, lightly beaten
2	onions, sliced		1	cup (4 ounces) grated Gruyère cheese
3	tablespoons butter			Nutmeg to taste
10	ounces fresh mushrooms, sliced			Salt and freshly ground pepper to taste
1/4	cup sherry		1	tablespoon chopped chives
1/4	cup heavy cream			
1	teaspoon fresh thyme leaves			

Press the pie pastry into a 9-inch tart pan and trim; prick with a fork. Bake at 450 degrees for 10 minutes. Cool to room temperature. Reduce the oven temperature to 375 degrees.

Sauté the onions in the butter in a skillet until translucent and beginning to brown. Add the mushrooms and wine and cook until the mushrooms are tender and most of the liquid has evaporated. Stir in the cream and thyme and remove from the heat. Add the eggs, cheese, nutmeg, salt and pepper; mix well.

Spoon into the prepared pie shell and sprinkle with the chives. Bake at 375 degrees for 20 minutes or until golden brown.

SERVES 8

Jalapeño Jack Cheese Grits

1/3	cup chopped red bell pepper		3	tablespoons butter
1/3	cup chopped green bell pepper		2	cups heavy cream
1/3	cup chopped yellow bell pepper		6	cups chicken stock
1	tablespoon chopped jalapeño chile		12	ounces uncooked grits
2	garlic cloves, crushed		1	cup (4 ounces) shredded pepper Jack cheese

Sauté the red bell pepper, green bell pepper, yellow bell pepper, jalapeño chile and garlic in the butter in a skillet. Bring the cream and chicken stock to a boil in a saucepan. Stir in the grits and reduce the heat. Add the sautéed vegetables and cook over low heat until thickened, stirring constantly. Add the cheese and cook until melted, stirring to mix well.

SERVES 6 TO 8

Award-Winning Plantation Dressing

20	slices stale white bread
1	pan stale corn bread, crumbled
1/2	cup (1 stick) unsalted butter
2	cups very finely chopped white or yellow onions
3	bunches green onions with tops, very finely chopped
2	cups very finely chopped celery
1	tablespoon (or more) salt
1	teaspoon (or more) pepper
4	cups (about) homemade chicken broth
1	pint shucked oysters, drained (optional)

Toast the white bread and tear into very small pieces. Combine with the corn bread in a large bowl.

Melt the butter in a skillet and add the onions, green onions and celery. Sauté until translucent. Add to the bread mixture and season with the salt and pepper. Add just enough of the chicken broth gradually to bind the mixture, checking by pressing the mixture with a spoon and stopping when the broth begins to seep into the bowl. Adjust the seasoning. Stir in the oysters.

Spoon into a large baking dish and cover with foil. Bake at 350 degrees for 30 minutes. Remove the foil and bake for 20 minutes longer or until the top is brown and the center is firm.

SERVES 12

Passing on Traditions

This recipe, submitted by Little Rock's Aylette Roper, was a top-five finalist in the Emeril Lagasse and Good Morning America's national search for the best Thanksgiving stuffing.
"Plantation Dressing has been in my family since before the Civil War and has been served every single holiday without any variance on the original recipe. My grandmother, who was a member of the Junior League of Little Rock, taught me how to make it. My great-grandmother was raised on Twin Oaks Plantation and her mother taught it to her, and so on. We know for a fact that this recipe is more than 150 years old. It has very few ingredients, but my grandmother sticks to the motto, 'Sometimes simpler is better.'"

—Aylette Roper

Grown-Up Mac and Cheese

12   *ounces turkey bacon*
1   *tablespoon vegetable oil*
     Salt to taste
16   *ounces uncooked macaroni*
4   *cups milk*
6   *tablespoons butter*
1/2 *cup all-purpose flour*
3   *cups (12 ounces) grated Gruyère cheese*
2 1/2 *cups (10 ounces) shredded extra-sharp Cheddar cheese*
1   *cup (4 ounces) crumbled blue cheese*
1   *tablespoon salt*
1/2 *teaspoon freshly ground pepper*
4   *slices white sandwich bread, crusts trimmed*
2   *tablespoons butter, melted*
1/4 *cup chopped fresh basil*

*A*rrange the bacon slices on a baking sheet and bake at 400 degrees for 15 to 20 minutes or until crisp. Drain and crumble coarsely. Reduce the oven temperature to 375 degrees.

Bring a large saucepan of water to a boil; add the oil and season with salt. Add the pasta and cook for 6 to 8 minutes or until al dente; drain.

Bring the milk just to a simmer in a saucepan and maintain at a simmer; do not boil. Melt 6 tablespoons butter in a large saucepan. Whisk in the flour. Cook for 2 minutes, whisking constantly. Add the hot milk and cook for 3 minutes or until thickened, whisking constantly.

Remove the sauce from the heat and add the Gruyère cheese, Cheddar cheese, blue cheese, 1 tablespoon salt and the pepper. Stir until the cheeses are melted and blended. Add the pasta and stir in the bacon. Spoon into six individual gratin dishes and place on two baking sheets.

Process the bread to coarse crumbs in a food processor. Mix with 2 tablespoons melted butter and the basil in a bowl. Sprinkle over the pasta. Bake at 350 degrees for 35 to 40 minutes or until golden brown.

SERVES 6

Curried Rice

1   cup uncooked brown or white basmati rice
1¹/2   cups water
¹/2   cup unsweetened light coconut milk
3   sprigs of rosemary
1¹/2   teaspoons curry powder
1   teaspoon salt
3   tablespoons golden raisins
³/4   cup frozen green peas
1   Granny Smith apple, sliced and cut into quarters
2   tablespoons sliced green onions
3   tablespoons chopped red bell pepper
       Thai Shrimp (page 123) (optional)
       Chopped parsley, for garnish

Combine the rice, water, coconut milk, rosemary, curry powder and salt in a 2-quart saucepan. Cover and bring to a boil over high heat. Reduce the heat to low and cook for 20 minutes using the directions on the rice package. Stir in the raisins, peas, apple, green onions and red bell pepper. Add additional water if needed. Cook, covered, for 5 minutes or until heated through. Remove from the heat and let stand, covered, for 5 minutes. Fluff with a fork. Serve topped with Thai Shrimp. Garnish with parsley.

SERVES 8

Grilled Corn on the Cob

Soak corn in its husks in water for 1 hour. Place the corn on a hot grill and grill for about 5 minutes. Carefully remove the husks and place the ears on a serving platter. Gently bruise four sprigs of fresh rosemary and dip into melted butter. Use the rosemary sprigs to brush the butter onto the ears of corn and serve immediately. You will taste the essence of the rosemary in every bite!

Green Rice Loaf

2   *cups cooked rice*
2   *cups (8 ounces) shredded Cheddar cheese*
1   *(4-ounce) can chopped green chiles*
1   *small onion, finely chopped*
1   *cup finely chopped fresh parsley*
1   *cup (2 sticks) butter, melted*
2   *eggs, lightly beaten*
1   *cup milk*

Combine the rice, cheese, green chiles, onion and parsley in a bowl and mix well. Stir in the melted butter. Mix the eggs with the milk in a bowl. Add to the rice mixture.

Line a greased 4×5-inch glass loaf pan with waxed paper; grease the waxed paper lightly. Spoon the rice mixture into the prepared pan. Bake at 350 degrees for 40 to 45 minutes or until set. Cool in the pan for several minutes and invert onto a serving plate. Cut into slices and serve warm.

SERVES 6

Franklin Delano Roosevelt in Little Rock

President Franklin Delano Roosevelt was the first president to visit Arkansas while in office. In June of 1936, he came to Little Rock to help celebrate our centennial of statehood and to visit with his close friend, United States Senator Joseph T. Robinson. After making a speech at the state capitol, the president went to Senator Robinson's home on Broadway for a reception and dinner. The two men had worked for years in the Democratic Party and, as Senate Majority Leader, Senator Robinson had been a major force for the president in gaining approval for his New Deal legislation. The Robinson home was designated a National Historic Landmark in 1994.

Creamy Lemon Risotto

4 cups chicken stock
3 shallots, minced
3 tablespoons butter
2 garlic cloves, minced
14 ounces uncooked arborio rice
Salt and freshly ground pepper to taste
1 cup vermouth
1/2 cup heavy cream
Juice and grated zest of 1 lemon
1/4 cup pine nuts
1/4 cup chopped flat-leaf Italian parsley

Bring the chicken stock to a simmer in a saucepan and maintain at a simmer. Sauté the shallots in the butter in a large skillet until translucent. Add the garlic and sauté for 1 minute. Stir in the rice, salt and pepper. Sauté for 1 minute or until the rice is slightly translucent, stirring constantly. Add the vermouth and cook until it has been absorbed.

Reduce the heat. Add the hot chicken stock one ladleful at a time, cooking until the liquid has been absorbed after each addition and the rice is creamy. Stir in the cream, lemon juice and lemon zest. Stir in the pine nuts and parsley and serve immediately.

SERVES 6

Apricot Wild Rice

2   packages wild rice mix
1   cup chopped dried apricots
1   cup boiling water
4   green onions, finely chopped
1/2 cup chopped green bell pepper
1   cup sliced mushrooms
2   garlic cloves, minced
1/2 cup (1 stick) butter
1/2 cup pecans, toasted
1/4 cup vermouth
2   tablespoons chopped fresh parsley
    Salt to taste
1/4 teaspoon pepper

Cook the rice using the package directions. Combine the dried apricots with the boiling water in a bowl and let stand for 20 minutes; drain.

Sauté the green onions, green bell pepper, mushrooms and garlic in the butter in a skillet over high heat until tender. Add the pecans and sauté until the pecans are fragrant. Add the rice, apricots, sautéed vegetables, vermouth, parsley, salt and pepper and mix well.

Spoon into a baking pan. Bake at 350 degrees for 30 minutes. This sweet and savory dish is good served with pork.

SERVES 8

Cooking with Wine

"The basic idea when adding wine to a dish is to get some specific flavors into the dish. A lot of wines have tasting notes on the back label. Pick a wine whose flavors work well with the dish. If you need Pepper and Jam, pick a zinfandel. If you need Strawberries and Banana, choose a beaujolais. If you want Cassis and Blackberry, use a cabernet. Trust tasting notes, and the dish should turn out fine. And price should never be a determining factor."

—Lee Edwards
President, Lee Edwards Distributing

Cranberry Orange Relish

1	navel orange	1	cup sugar
16	ounces fresh cranberries	2	tablespoons Grand Marnier or
1	large Granny Smith apple, cored		Triple Sec
	and coarsely chopped		

*C*ut the unpeeled orange into eight wedges. Combine with the cranberries, apple, sugar and liqueur in a food processor. Process until finely chopped. Spoon into a bowl and store in the refrigerator. Serve cold.

SERVES 4

Squash Relish

5	cups chopped yellow squash	1	teaspoon cornstarch
2	cups chopped onions	1	teaspoon turmeric
1	cup chopped green bell pepper	1	teaspoon celery seeds
2^1/$_2$	tablespoons salt	1	teaspoon dry mustard
1^1/$_4$	cups apple cider vinegar	^{1}/$_4$	teaspoon nutmeg
2	cups sugar	^{1}/$_4$	teaspoon pepper

*M*ix the squash, onions, green bell pepper and salt in a large bowl. Let stand at room temperature for 1 hour. Drain, rinse and drain again.

Combine the vegetables with the vinegar, sugar, cornstarch, turmeric, celery seeds, dry mustard, nutmeg and pepper in a large saucepan. Bring to a simmer and cook for 20 minutes. Spoon into three 1-pint jars and seal. Store in the refrigerator. Serve with black-eyed peas or on a sandwich.

MAKES 3 PINTS

Brunch &
Breads

Sample the Past

Little Rock Central High School

The 1957–1958 desegregation crisis at Little Rock Central High School made our community the site of the first important test of the U.S. Supreme Court's historic *Brown v. Board of Education of Topeka* decision. With courage and conviction, the nine African-American students who desegregated the school have been honored as pioneers of the civil rights movement. That event is chronicled at the National Park Service's Visitors Center located adjacent to the school. Today LRCHS is the only functioning high school designated as a National Historic Site. Built more than eight decades ago, Little Rock Central is considered one of the most beautiful schools in America and academically, has been ranked recently in the top twenty-five high schools in the U.S. by *Newsweek*. Central High is honored for its place in history, and it continues to give the children of Central Arkansas a taste of a bright future.

Café Smoothie

3/4 cup espresso or very strong coffee, chilled
1 teaspoon caramel syrup
1 to 1¹/2 cups vanilla frozen yogurt
2 teaspoons hazelnut flavoring
  Chopped hazelnuts, for garnish

Process the espresso, caramel syrup, yogurt and hazelnut flavoring in a blender until smooth. Pour into small cups and garnish with chopped hazelnuts.

SERVES 4

Chocolate Orange Smoothie

1 cup light vanilla yogurt
1 cup skim milk
1/4 cup frozen orange juice concentrate
2 to 3 tablespoons chocolate syrup
1 to 2 teaspoons grated orange zest
2 to 4 cups ice

Place the yogurt, skim milk, frozen orange juice concentrate, chocolate syrup and orange zest in a blender. Add enough ice to fill the blender. Process until smooth.

SERVES 2 OR 3

Little Rock Nine

While it was nine justices of the United States Supreme Court in Washington, D.C., who heard the case of Brown v. Board of Education, *it was nine students who epitomized the impact of the* Brown *decision in the fall of 1957. Known as the Little Rock Nine, the group included Melba Pattillo, Elizabeth Eckford, Ernest Green, Gloria Ray, Carlotta Walls, Terrence Roberts, Jefferson Thomas, Minnijean Brown, and Thelma Mothershed. As they were in 1957, these pioneers are honored with life-size bronze statues on the grounds of the capitol. This tribute was created by Little Rock artists Cathy and John Deering. In 1999, members of the Little Rock Nine were awarded the Congressional Gold Medal, the highest civilian award bestowed by the U.S. Congress.*

Strawberry Sunrise Smoothie

1 (16-ounce) package frozen strawberries	1/2 cup plain yogurt
2 bananas, coarsely chopped	2 tablespoons honey
1 1/2 cups orange juice	1 teaspoon vanilla extract

*C*ombine the strawberries and bananas in a blender. Add the orange juice, yogurt, honey and vanilla and process until smooth.

SERVES 4

Healthy Granola

1 1/2 cups unsalted sunflower seeds	1 teaspoon vanilla extract
2/3 cup sesame seeds	1/4 teaspoon salt
1 1/2 cups unsalted slivered almonds	8 cups rolled oats
1/2 cup vegetable oil	3/4 to 1 cup shredded coconut
1 cup honey	(optional)
1/2 cup packed brown sugar	

*S*prinkle the sunflower seeds and sesame seeds in an ovenproof skillet. Toast at 300 degrees just until light golden brown, stirring occasionally. Remove to a bowl. Sprinkle the almonds in the skillet and toast until light golden brown. Do not overtoast the seeds and almonds, as they will continue to cook with the granola. Increase the oven temperature to 350 degrees.

Combine the oil, honey and brown sugar in a saucepan. Cook over low heat for 5 minutes or until the brown sugar has melted, stirring to blend well. Remove from the heat and stir in the vanilla and salt.

Pour the honey mixture over the oats in a bowl. Add the toasted almonds and seeds and mix well. Spread evenly in two baking pans. Bake at 350 degrees for 10 minutes or until brown, stirring every 5 minutes. Add the coconut and bake for 5 minutes or just until the coconut is brown, watching carefully as it will brown quickly.

Store in an airtight container or sealable plastic bag. Serve with yogurt and fruit or milk as cereal, or place in decorative jars for great homemade gifts.

MAKES 12 CUPS

Sunrise Service Easter Brunch

Crostini with Goat Cheese and Walnuts

20

Orange and Hearts of Palm Salad

61

Cold Poached Salmon with Cucumber Dill Sauce

169

Benedict Bake

174

Tiny Orange Muffins with Orange Curd

194

Marinated Asparagus

129

Almond Peach Trifle

231

Wine: French Sauvignon Blanc (non-oaked)

Cold Poached Salmon with Cucumber Dill Sauce

6	cups water	6	(7- to 8-ounce) center-cut salmon
2¹/2	cups white wine		fillets, skin removed
6	lemon slices		Salt and white pepper to taste
2	sprigs of fresh thyme		Cucumber Dill Sauce (below)

*P*our half the water and wine into each of two large skillets. Add half the lemon slices and thyme to each skillet. Bring to a boil and turn off the heat.

Season the salmon with salt and white pepper. Place three fillets in each skillet and let stand for 6 minutes. Turn the fillets and let stand for 5 minutes longer.

Bring the liquid in the skillets to a simmer and cook for 30 seconds or just until the salmon is cooked through.

Remove the salmon to a platter with a slotted spatula. Chill, covered, in the refrigerator for 3 to 24 hours. Let stand at room temperature for 1 hour before serving. Serve with the Cucumber Dill Sauce.

SERVES 6

Cucumber Dill Sauce

¹/2	cup plain yogurt	1	teaspoon minced garlic
¹/2	cup sour cream	1	tablespoon olive oil
¹/2	cup grated peeled cucumber,	1	teaspoon lemon juice
	squeezed to remove	1	tablespoon minced fresh dill
	excess moisture		Salt and pepper to taste

*C*ombine the yogurt, sour cream, cucumber and garlic in a food processor and process until smooth. Combine with the olive oil, lemon juice and dill in a bowl. Season with salt and pepper and mix well. Store, covered, in the refrigerator until serving time.

MAKES 1¹/2 CUPS

Apple Sandwiches

2   unpeeled apples
     Juice of 1 orange
8   ounces cream cheese, softened
1/2 cup packed brown sugar
1   teaspoon vanilla extract
2   loaves cinnamon-raisin bread
1/2 cup crushed peanuts

Core the apples and cut each into six rings. Dip in the orange juice to prevent browning. Combine the cream cheese, brown sugar and vanilla in a bowl and mix well. Spread the cream cheese mixture over the slices of one loaf of bread.

Place one apple slice on each slice of bread and sprinkle with the peanuts. Top with the remaining bread. Chill, covered, for 2 to 12 hours. Cut into halves diagonally.

SERVES 12

A Change Worth the Risk

"As we all know, Little Rock Central High School has become one of the most recognized public high schools in the world. It was thrust into the history books much as I was—unexpectedly.
But, this exposure over the last fifty years has given LRCHS an opportunity to represent the changes and growth that American society has achieved. These changes span from resistance and denial to embracing the multicultural and diverse society we have become. I hope that the JLLR cookbook continues to build on this expansion and that Little Rock Central High School will continue to represent the changing positive qualities that are important for our future. In 1957 I saw this building as a new opportunity, even with its inherent problems. I believed then it represented a brighter future and it was worth the risk. Today fifty years later, I believe I made the right choice. Hopefully, Little Rock Central High School will always represent opportunity and a brighter future for every student that goes through her doors."

—Ernest G. Green
LRCHS graduate and member of the Little Rock Nine

Apple Bacon Sausage Balls

1/2 cup (1 stick) margarine
1   cup water
3   cups herb-seasoned stuffing mix
4   ounces breakfast sausage, crumbled

4   ounces turkey sausage, crumbled
1/4 cup shredded apple
2   cups chopped pecans
1 to 2 pounds sliced bacon

Heat the margarine in the water in a saucepan until melted. Add to the stuffing mix in a bowl and mix well. Add the breakfast sausage, turkey sausage and apple; mix well. Chill for 1 hour. Shape by tablespoonfuls into balls and roll each ball in the chopped pecans. Cut the bacon slices crosswise into thirds. Wrap one piece of bacon around each ball and secure with a wooden pick. Place on a baking sheet and bake at 350 degrees for 35 to 45 minutes or until cooked through. You can cut one of the balls into halves to test for doneness. This can also be served as an appetizer.

SERVES 8

Delta Breakfast Bars

2   (8-count) cans refrigerator crescent rolls
1   pound hot pork sausage
1/4 cup minced onion
8   ounces fresh mushrooms
1   (4-ounce) can chopped green chiles

1   teaspoon fresh thyme
8   ounces cream cheese, chopped
1   egg white, lightly beaten
     Poppy seeds to taste

Open one can of the crescent roll dough and press it over the bottom of a baking dish, pressing the perforations to seal. Brown the sausage in a large skillet, stirring until crumbly. Add the onion and sauté until tender. Add the mushrooms, green chiles and thyme. Sauté until the mushrooms are tender; drain. Add the cream cheese to the vegetables in the skillet and cook until melted and smooth, stirring constantly. Spread the mixture over the roll dough.

Open the second can of roll dough and separate into triangles. Arrange the triangles over the sausage mixture, leaving a small space between triangles. Brush with the egg white and sprinkle with poppy seeds. Bake at 375 degrees for 30 minutes or until golden brown.

SERVES 12

Baked Herbed Eggs

1/2 teaspoon minced garlic
1/2 teaspoon fresh thyme
1/2 teaspoon fresh rosemary
1 tablespoon chopped parsley
1 tablespoon grated Parmesan cheese
4 eggs
2 tablespoons cream
1 tablespoon butter
Salt and pepper to taste

Combine the garlic, thyme, rosemary, parsley and cheese in a small bowl and mix well. Break two eggs into each of two glasses. Place two individual gratin dishes on a baking sheet. Place 1 tablespoon of cream and 1/2 tablespoon of butter in each dish. Broil for 3 minutes or until bubbly.

Pour the eggs gently into the gratin dishes and season each with salt and pepper. Top each with half the herb mixture. Broil for 3 minutes. Rotate the baking sheet and broil for 3 minutes longer. Serve with Orange and Hearts of Palm Salad on page 61 and Focaccia on page 196.

SERVES 2

Women's Emergency Committee to Open Our Schools

In September of 1958, the Women's Emergency Committee to Open Our Schools came together to support the reopening of the schools under Little Rock's plan to integrate schools. These women, many of whom were members of JLLR, actively campaigned to win the support of the citizens of Little Rock to back the school district's plan for integration. This support of public education continues today as the Junior League of Little Rock is recognized by the Little Rock School District as a member of its organization, Volunteers in Public Schools (VIPS), and through our community projects Stuff the Bus, Buckle Up and Be Safe, and Girls Realizing Opportunity Within (GROW).

Benedict Bake

2   envelopes hollandaise sauce mix
2   cups half-and-half
1/4   cup (1/2 stick) butter, melted
12   eggs
1 1/2   cups (6 ounces) grated Gruyère cheese
8   ounces Canadian bacon, chopped
1   (10-ounce) package frozen chopped spinach,
      cooked and well drained
2   tablespoons lemon juice
      Salt and freshly ground pepper to taste
6   English muffins, cut into cubes

Combine the hollandaise sauce mix, half-and-half and melted butter in a large mixing bowl and whisk until smooth. Add the eggs and beat until smooth. Stir in the cheese, Canadian bacon, spinach and lemon juice. Season with salt and pepper.

Sprinkle the English muffin cubes in a baking pan. Pour the egg mixture over the English muffins. Chill in the refrigerator for 8 hours or longer. Bake at 350 degrees for 45 minutes or until light brown on top.

SERVES 8

Maple Sausage Breakfast Ring

1   pound hot sausage
1   pound mild sausage
1 1/2   cups cracker crumbs
2   eggs, beaten
1/2   cup milk
1/2   cup finely chopped apple
1/4   cup maple syrup
1   tablespoon chopped fresh sage
16   eggs, scrambled

Brown the hot sausage and mild sausage in a skillet, stirring until crumbly; drain. Combine with the cracker crumbs, beaten eggs, milk, apple, maple syrup and sage in a large bowl. Spoon into a greased ring mold. Bake at 350 degrees for 35 to 40 minutes or until set. Invert onto a serving platter and fill the center with the scrambled eggs.

SERVES 12

South-of-the-Border Breakfast Casserole

1¹/2 pounds hot sausage
1   cup chopped onion
¹/2   cup chopped red bell pepper
4   garlic cloves, minced
2   (4-ounce) cans chopped green chiles
1   tablespoon chili powder
1¹/2 teaspoons cumin
8   corn tortillas, cut into quarters
1¹/2 cups (6 ounces) shredded pepper Jack cheese
1¹/2 cups (6 ounces) shredded Cheddar cheese
¹/2   cup chopped green onion tops
¹/2   cup chopped cilantro
1   large tomato, sliced
10   eggs
2¹/2 cups half-and-half
¹/2   teaspoon hot sauce
¹/2   teaspoon salt
¹/2   teaspoon pepper

Brown the sausage in a skillet, stirring until crumbly. Add the onion, red bell pepper and garlic. Sauté until the vegetables are tender. Stir in the green chiles, chili powder and cumin and sauté for 1 minute.

Layer the sausage mixture, tortillas, pepper Jack cheese, Cheddar cheese, green onion tops and cilantro one-half at a time in a greased 9×13-inch baking dish. Top with the tomato slices.

Beat the eggs with the half-and-half, hot sauce, salt and pepper in a bowl. Pour over the layers. Chill, covered, for 8 hours or longer. Bake at 350 degrees for 1¹/4 hours or until golden brown.

SERVES 10

Sausage and Pepper Quiche

1 pound hot sausage	1/2 cup mayonnaise
1/2 red bell pepper, chopped	1 cup (4 ounces) shredded
1/2 green bell pepper, chopped	Cheddar cheese
1/2 onion, chopped	1 tablespoon cornstarch
1 unbaked (9-inch) pie shell	1/2 cup milk
2 eggs	Salt and pepper to taste

Brown the sausage with the red bell pepper, green bell pepper and onion in a skillet, stirring until the sausage is crumbly; drain. Spoon into the pie shell.

Combine the eggs, mayonnaise, cheese, cornstarch and milk in a bowl and mix well. Season with salt and pepper. Pour over the sausage mixture in the pie shell. Bake at 350 degrees for 40 minutes or until set and golden brown.

Men love this hearty variation of quiche. You can vary it with the addition of cumin and/or chili powder, reduced-fat sausage or other cheeses.

SERVES 8

Crab Meat Quiche

1/2 cup mayonnaise	2 cups lump crab meat
2 tablespoons all-purpose flour	8 ounces Swiss cheese, chopped
2 eggs, beaten	1/3 cup sliced green onions
1/2 cup milk	1 unbaked pie shell

Whisk the mayonnaise, flour, eggs and milk in a bowl until smooth. Fold in the crab meat, cheese and green onions. Spoon into the pie shell. Bake at 350 degrees for 40 to 45 minutes or until set and light brown.

SERVES 4 OR 5

Crustless Spinach Quiche

1	cup chopped onion	2/3	cup finely chopped cooked ham
1	cup sliced fresh mushrooms	5	eggs
1	tablespoon vegetable oil	3	cups (12 ounces) shredded
1	(10-ounce) package frozen		Monterey Jack cheese
	spinach, thawed and		Salt and pepper to taste
	well drained		

Sauté the onion and mushrooms in the oil in a large skillet until tender. Add the spinach and ham and cook until the moisture has evaporated.

Beat the eggs in a bowl and add the cheese; mix well. Stir in the spinach mixture and season with salt and pepper.

Spoon into a greased 9-inch pie plate. Bake at 350 degrees for 40 to 45 minutes or until set.

SERVES 6 TO 8

Grilled Fruit Kabobs

2	cups fresh pineapple chunks	3	tablespoons honey
2	pears, cored and cut into chunks	2	tablespoons chopped fresh mint
2	apricots, cut into quarters	1/2	cup vegetable oil
2	plums, cut into quarters		Chopped fresh mint, for garnish
1/2	cup balsamic vinegar		

Thread the pineapple, pears, apricots and plums onto six skewers. Combine the vinegar, honey and 2 tablespoons mint in a bowl. Whisk in the oil gradually. Brush half the vinegar mixture over the fruit.

Grill for 2 to 3 minutes or until the sugars begin to caramelize and the fruit is marked by the grill. Drizzle with the remaining vinegar mixture. Garnish with additional mint.

SERVES 6

Basil-Stuffed Tomatoes

3   tomatoes
2/3   cup saltine cracker crumbs
2/3   cup butter-flavor cracker crumbs
1   cup cooked drained sausage (optional)
1/2   cup (1 stick) butter, melted
1   tablespoon fresh lemon juice
1/4   cup capers, drained
2   tablespoons chopped basil
1/2   teaspoon paprika
1   teaspoon celery salt

Remove the stem ends of the tomatoes and cut the tomatoes into halves crosswise. Scoop out the tomato pulp, reserving the pulp and shells; discard the seeds. Arrange the shells cut side up in a baking dish.

Chop the scooped-out portion of the tomatoes. Combine with the saltine cracker crumbs, butter-flavor cracker crumbs, sausage, butter, lemon juice, capers, basil, paprika and celery salt in a bowl; mix well.

Spoon the sausage mixture into the tomato halves. Bake at 350 degrees for 15 to 20 minutes or until the stuffing is golden brown.

SERVES 6

Artichoke and Bacon Grits

1   cup uncooked grits
1   (14-ounce) can chicken broth
1/4 cup water
2   tablespoons butter
8   slices bacon, crisp-cooked and crumbled
1   (14-ounce) can artichoke hearts, drained and chopped
1   cup (4 ounces) grated Parmesan cheese
3   tablespoons sour cream
2   eggs, beaten
1/2 teaspoon cayenne pepper
    Salt and black pepper to taste

Cook the grits in the chicken broth and water in a saucepan using the package directions. Add the butter and stir until melted. Add the bacon, artichoke hearts and cheese and mix well.

Combine the sour cream and eggs in a bowl and mix well. Add to the grits with the cayenne pepper and mix well. Season with salt and black pepper. Spoon into a greased baking dish. Bake at 350 degrees for 45 minutes.

SERVES 6

Little Rock Central High School Today

*"Characterizing Little Rock Central High School is like seeking to define an emotion.
With a sense of urgency, students, teachers, and staff seek daily to aim to be the very best they can be.
With dedicated purpose, we are focused on making LRCHS a continuing source of excellence and
pride. With determined spirit, we strive to compete successfully with world-class academic standards,
championship athletics, and unmatched extracurricular programs. With historic legacies, we
cherish the contributions our institution has made in advancing America. Without question, for over
eighty years, we are Tigers who have genuinely earned our stripes."*

—Nancy Rousseau
Principal, Little Rock Central High School

Almond Strata

6   large croissants
8   eggs, lightly beaten
2   cups sugar
3   cups half-and-half
1   tablespoon amaretto
2   teaspoons vanilla extract
1/4   cup almond paste, cut into small pieces
1/2   cup slivered almonds, toasted

Cut the croissants crosswise into 1/2-inch slices. Arrange the smaller slices in a buttered 9×13-inch baking pan. Arrange the larger slices over the top.

Combine the eggs and sugar in a bowl and whisk until smooth. Add the half-and-half, liqueur and vanilla and mix well. Pour over the croissant slices and sprinkle with the almond paste. Press down with a spoon to submerge the bread completely. Let stand at room temperature for 10 minutes.

Sprinkle the almonds over the top. Bake at 350 degrees for 35 to 40 minutes or until puffed and golden brown. Serve warm or at room temperature with fresh berries.

SERVES 8

Tea Cakes with Clotted Cream and Jam

2   cups plus 6 tablespoons all-purpose flour
1   teaspoon baking powder
1/2   teaspoon baking soda
1/2   teaspoon salt
1/2   cup shortening
1   cup sugar
2   eggs
1   tablespoon milk
1   teaspoon vanilla extract
     Sugar for sprinkling
     Clotted Cream (see below)

Sift the flour, baking powder, baking soda and salt into a large bowl. Cut in the shortening. Combine 1 cup sugar with the eggs, milk and vanilla in a bowl and mix well. Add the flour mixture gradually, mixing well after each addition.

Roll on a lightly floured surface and cut with a biscuit cutter. Arrange on a baking sheet. Bake at 350 degrees for 8 to 10 minutes. Sprinkle with additional sugar.

Serve with Clotted Cream and jam.

This is a very versatile recipe. You can vary the flavor with different extracts, such as lemon, almond, orange, or mint. It can be used for strawberry shortcake. It also makes a great gift to include in a basket of goodies.

MAKES ABOUT 2 DOZEN

Clotted Cream

Clotted cream is a decadent spread to serve with any biscuit, scone, or tea cake. To prepare, line a coffee filter basket with a paper filter and set in a strainer over a bowl. Pour two cups of pasteurized cream almost to the top of the filter and place in the refrigerator for two hours. The whey will pass through the filter to the bottom and leave a ring of clotted cream. Scrape down the ring every couple of hours until the mass reaches the consistency of a soft cream cheese.

Arkansas Muscadine Preserves

5   quarts muscadine grapes
2¹/₂ cups (or more) sugar

*P*ierce the grape skins with a sharp knife and squeeze the pulp into a saucepan. Place the skins in a second saucepan. Cook the pulp and the skins over low heat for 10 to 15 minutes or until tender, stirring frequently.

Press the pulp through a sieve to remove the seeds. Add to the saucepan with the skins. Add the sugar. Cook over low heat for 15 to 20 minutes or until of the desired consistency. Spoon into sterilized jars and seal. Store in the refrigerator.

MAKES 6 (1-PINT) JARS

Muscadines

*Muscadine grapes have thick greenish-purple skins and a sweet musky flavor.
They usually arrive at Farmers' Market in mid-August in Arkansas and make great preserves
for fall. The preserves are a great addition to the table at Thanksgiving with
turkey and dressing but are also wonderful on hot toast or English muffins for breakfast.*

Sour Cream Coffee Cake

1 cup (2 sticks) butter or margarine, softened
2 cups plus 4 teaspoons granulated sugar
2 eggs
1 cup sour cream
2 cups all-purpose flour
1 teaspoon baking powder
1 teaspoon vanilla extract
$^1/_4$ teaspoon salt
$^1/_4$ cup packed brown sugar
1 cup pecans, finely chopped
$^1/_2$ teaspoon cinnamon

Cream the butter in a mixing bowl until light. Add the granulated sugar and beat until fluffy. Beat in the eggs. Add the sour cream, flour, baking powder, vanilla and salt and mix well.

Combine the brown sugar, pecans and cinnamon in a bowl and mix well. Grease a bundt pan and sprinkle with some of the brown sugar mixture, shaking out and reserving the excess.

Layer the batter and remaining brown sugar mixture one-half at a time in the prepared bundt pan, pressing the top layer of brown sugar lightly into the batter. Bake at 350 degrees for 60 to 65 minutes or until the coffee cake tests done. Cool in the pan for several minutes. Invert onto a wire rack to cool completely.

SERVES 10 TO 12

French Toast Brûlée with Praline Syrup

4 1/2 cups heavy cream
8 egg yolks
3/4 cup sugar
2 tablespoons maple syrup
2 tablespoons butter, melted
2 tablespoons vanilla extract

1/2 teaspoon salt
1 loaf challah, cut into
 bite-size pieces
3 to 4 tablespoons sugar
 Praline Syrup (below)

Whisk the cream, egg yolks, 3/4 cup sugar, the maple syrup, melted butter, vanilla and salt in a large bowl until smooth.

Sprinkle one-fourth of the bread cubes in a greased 2 1/2-quart soufflé dish. Add about one-fourth of the cream mixture or enough to cover the bread; press the bread into the cream mixture with a spoon. Repeat the layers until all the ingredients are used, pressing each layer of bread into the cream mixture. Cover tightly with foil and chill for 1 to 12 hours.

Place the soufflé dish in a baking pan with tall sides. Add enough boiling water to the baking pan to reach halfway up the side of the soufflé dish. Bake at 325 degrees for 1 1/2 hours or until the mixture is set and the top is light brown.

Sprinkle 3 to 4 tablespoons sugar evenly over the top. Place a few inches from the heat source and broil at high heat until the sugar melts and browns. You can also melt the sugar with a kitchen torch if preferred. Serve at room temperature with Praline Syrup.

SERVES 8 TO 10

Praline Syrup

1 cup maple syrup
1/4 cup (1/2 stick) butter
1/4 cup packed brown sugar

1 cup chopped pecans
1 teaspoon vanilla extract

Combine the maple syrup, butter, brown sugar and pecans in a small saucepan and mix well. Cook over medium heat until the butter and brown sugar melt, stirring to mix well. Remove from the heat and stir in the vanilla.

MAKES 2 1/2 CUPS

Puffed Blueberry French Toast

4 ounces cream cheese, softened
1 loaf French bread
1/2 cup blueberry jam
8 eggs, lightly beaten
1 cup heavy cream
1 1/2 teaspoons vanilla extract
Blueberry Syrup (below)

Combine the cream cheese and blueberry jam in a bowl and mix until smooth. Cut the bread into twenty 1-inch slices. Spread the cream cheese mixture over ten slices of the bread and top with the remaining bread. Arrange in a shallow dish.

Combine the eggs, cream and vanilla in a bowl and whisk until smooth. Pour over the bread, turning several times to coat well. Chill, covered, in the refrigerator for 8 to 12 hours.

Remove the bread to a lightly greased shallow baking dish with a spatula. Bake at 375 degrees for 20 to 25 minutes or until puffed and golden brown. Serve with Blueberry Syrup.

SERVES 10

Blueberry Syrup

2 cups maple syrup
1 cup blueberries
1 tablespoon butter

Place the maple syrup and blueberries in a saucepan. Cook over medium heat for 5 minutes or until most of the blueberries have burst, stirring constantly. Stir in the butter.

MAKES 3 CUPS

Oatmeal Pancake Mix

4	cups rolled oats	3	tablespoons baking powder
2	cups all-purpose flour	2	teaspoons cinnamon
2	cups whole wheat flour	1/2	teaspoon cream of tartar
1	cup packed brown sugar	5	teaspoons salt
1	cup instant nonfat dry milk powder		

Combine the oats, all-purpose flour, whole wheat flour, brown sugar, dry milk powder, baking powder, cinnamon, cream of tartar and salt in a large bowl and mix well. Store in an airtight container.

MAKES 10 CUPS

Oatmeal Pancakes

2	cups Oatmeal Pancake Mix (above)	1/3	cup canola oil
2	eggs	1	cup water
			Applesauce Topping (see below)

Mix the pancake mix, eggs, canola oil and water in a bowl. Ladle onto a lightly greased nonstick griddle and cook until light brown on both sides. Serve with Applesauce Topping.

MAKES 10 PANCAKES

Applesauce Topping

Make Oatmeal Pancakes even more comforting by topping them with homemade Applesauce Topping. Just cook one-half pound of peeled and chopped apples in a saucepan over medium heat for 30 minutes or until tender. Add one-half cup of packed brown sugar, three-fourths teaspoon of cinnamon, and one-fourth teaspoon each of cloves and allspice. Mash until the desired consistency is reached. Serve warm.

Sweet Potato Biscuits with Cinnamon Butter

2   *cups hot mashed sweet potatoes*
1/2 cup shortening
3/4 cup sugar
7   tablespoons buttermilk
3 to 4 cups all-purpose flour
4   teaspoons baking powder
1/2 teaspoon baking soda
1   teaspoon salt
Cinnamon Butter (see below)

Combine the sweet potatoes and shortening in a large bowl and mix until the shortening melts and the mixture is smooth. Add the sugar and buttermilk and mix well. Sift in 3 cups of the flour, the baking powder, baking soda and salt; stir to mix well. Add enough of the remaining flour to make a stiff dough.

Roll the dough 1/2 inch thick on a lightly floured surface; cut with a 2-inch cutter. Place on a baking sheet and bake at 450 degrees for 20 minutes or until light brown.

Serve with Cinnamon Butter.

SERVES 12

Cinnamon Butter

Combine one-half cup of softened butter, one cup of honey, and one teaspoon of cinnamon in a mixing bowl. Beat until light and fluffy and place in your favorite serving dish. Cinnamon Butter may also be formed into shapes by using a decorator bag fitted with a star tip. Simply pipe the butter onto a baking parchment-lined baking sheet and chill in the refrigerator until serving time.

BLT Biscuits

1   (10-count) can refrigerator biscuits
$1/3$ cup mayonnaise
8   slices bacon, crisp-cooked and crumbled
$1/4$ cup coarsely chopped basil leaves
$1/4$ teaspoon kosher salt
$1/4$ teaspoon freshly ground pepper
2   tomatoes, sliced

Flatten each biscuit into a 4-inch circle and place on a baking sheet. Bake at 400 degrees for 6 minutes. Combine the mayonnaise, bacon, basil, kosher salt and pepper in a bowl and mix well. Spread over the biscuits. Top each with a tomato slice and bake for 6 minutes longer. Serve immediately.

SERVES 10

Central High School Fiftieth Anniversary

On September 25, 1957, the world watched as nine African-American students entered Little Rock Central High School. By desegregating the school, they not only walked through the front doors; they also walked into the history books. On September 25, 2007, the fiftieth anniversary of that historic occasion was commemorated, as the past was remembered, the present was examined, and the future was anticipated. History was made again when—for the first time ever—each member of the Little Rock Nine spoke at the same public event. With President Bill Clinton and U.S. Senator Hillary Rodham Clinton participating, this program was the culmination of more than two hundred activities throughout Little Rock and the United States.

Chipotle Stone-Ground Corn Bread

6	slices smoked bacon	1/4	cup vegetable oil
1 1/2	cups stone-ground yellow cornmeal	2	cups buttermilk
		1	cup whole kernel corn
3	tablespoons all-purpose flour	1	cup (4 ounces) shredded Monterey Jack cheese
1	teaspoon baking soda		
1	teaspoon salt	1 or 2 canned chipotle chiles, drained and finely chopped	
1	egg		

Cook the bacon in a 10-inch cast-iron skillet until crisp. Remove and crumble the bacon, reserving the drippings in the skillet. Tilt the skillet to coat the bottom and side with the drippings and place in an oven preheated to 450 degrees. Heat for 5 minutes or until very hot.

Mix the cornmeal, flour, baking soda and salt in a medium bowl. Add the egg and oil and mix well. Add the buttermilk just before removing the skillet from the oven and mix until smooth. Fold in the corn, cheese, chipotle chiles and bacon.

Remove the skillet from the oven and pour off any excess drippings. Pour the batter into the hot skillet and bake for 25 to 30 minutes or until set and golden brown.

SERVES 8

Cheese and Sausage Bread

1	pound hot sausage	1/2	teaspoon salt
1/2	cup finely chopped onion	2	cups baking mix (tested with Bisquick)
1	cup (4 ounces) shredded Swiss cheese		
		1	egg
2	tablespoons finely chopped fresh parsley	2/3	cup milk
		1/4	cup mayonnaise
	Tabasco sauce to taste		

Brown the sausage with the onion in a skillet, stirring until the sausage is crumbly; drain. Add the cheese, parsley, Tabasco sauce and salt and mix well.

Combine the baking mix, egg, milk and mayonnaise in a bowl and mix well. Spoon half the batter into a greased 8×8-inch baking pan. Spread with the sausage mixture and top with the remaining batter. Bake at 350 degrees for 30 minutes.

SERVES 8

Applesauce Bread

1 cup raisins	1/2 teaspoon salt
1 cup chopped nuts	1/4 cup (1/2 stick) butter, softened
1 3/4 cups cake flour	1 cup packed brown sugar
1 teaspoon baking soda	1 egg
1 teaspoon cinnamon	1 cup lightly sweetened applesauce
1/2 teaspoon cloves	

Toss the raisins and nuts with 1/4 cup of the flour in a plastic bag or paper bag until coated. Place in a sifter over a bowl and shake to remove the excess flour, reserving the flour.

Combine the reserved flour with the remaining 1 1/2 cups flour. Sift the flour, baking soda, cinnamon, cloves and salt into a bowl.

Cream the butter in a mixing bowl for 2 to 3 minutes or until light. Add the brown sugar gradually, beating constantly for 1 minute or until fluffy. Beat in the egg. Add the flour mixture alternately with the applesauce, beginning and ending with the flour and beating at the lowest speed until smooth. Fold in the raisin mixture with a spatula.

Spoon into a greased and floured 5×9-inch loaf pan. Bake at 350 degrees for 45 to 50 minutes or until a wooden pick inserted in the center comes out clean. Cool in the pan for several minutes. Remove to a wire rack to cool completely.

SERVES 12

Brewery Bread

3 cups self-rising flour
1/2 cup sugar
1 (12-ounce) can beer
1/2 cup (1 stick) butter, melted

Combine the flour, sugar and beer in a bowl and mix until smooth. Spoon into a greased loaf pan. Bake at 350 degrees for 45 minutes. Pour the melted butter over the top and bake for 10 minutes longer. Cool in the pan for several minutes. Remove to a wire rack to cool completely.

SERVES 12

Butternut Squash Bread

1   large butternut squash
1¹/2   cups self-rising flour
³/4   cup granulated sugar
¹/2   cup packed dark brown sugar
1   teaspoon ground nutmeg
1   teaspoon cinnamon
¹/2   cup canola oil
2   eggs, beaten
2   tablespoons water
1   teaspoon fresh lemon juice
1   teaspoon vanilla extract
¹/2   cup chopped pecans

Roast the butternut squash at 375 degrees for 1 hour or until tender. Cut the squash into halves; scoop out and discard the seeds. Scoop out and measure 1 cup of the cooked pulp.

Mix the flour, granulated sugar, brown sugar, nutmeg and cinnamon in a bowl. Combine the squash with the canola oil, eggs, water, lemon juice and vanilla in a bowl and mix well. Fold into the dry ingredients. Fold in the pecans.

Spoon into a greased 5×9-inch loaf pan. Bake at 350 degrees for 1 hour and 10 minutes or until a wooden pick inserted into the center comes out clean. Cool in the pan for several minutes. Remove to a wire rack to cool completely.

You can substitute zucchini or pumpkin for the butternut squash in this recipe.

SERVES 6 TO 8

Cranberry Bread

2   cups sifted all-purpose flour
1   cup sugar
1¹/2 teaspoons baking powder
¹/2   teaspoon baking soda
1   teaspoon salt
¹/4   cup (¹/2 stick) butter
1   egg, beaten
¹/4   cup (¹/2 stick) butter, melted and cooled
³/4   cup orange juice
1   teaspoon grated orange zest
1¹/2 cups fresh or frozen cranberries, chopped

Sift the flour, sugar, baking powder, baking soda and salt into a large bowl. Cut in ¹/4 cup butter until the mixture is crumbly. Add the egg, melted butter, orange juice and orange zest and stir just until moistened. Fold in the cranberries.

Spoon into a greased 5×9-inch loaf pan. Bake at 350 degrees for 1 hour or until a wooden pick inserted into the center comes out clean. Cool in the pan for several minutes. Remove to a wire rack to cool completely.

SERVES 8

The Daisy Bates House

Daisy Lee Gaston Bates of Little Rock was one of the most prominent national leaders of the civil rights movement. She served as president of the Arkansas State Conference of the NAACP branches and was instrumental in enforcing federal court decisions relating to schools. During the 1957–1958 crisis, the Bateses' home was the official pick-up and drop-off point for the nine students involved in the desegregation of Little Rock Central High School. Located at 1207 West 28th Street, the house has been designated as a National Historic Landmark and is private property not open to the public.

Tiny Orange Muffins with Orange Curd

3	cups all-purpose flour	2	eggs, lightly beaten
1	cup sugar	1	cup buttermilk
2	teaspoons baking powder		Grated zest of 2 oranges
1	teaspoon baking soda		Grated zest of 1 lemon
1/2	teaspoon salt	1	cup chopped nuts (optional)
1/2	cup (1 stick) butter, softened		Orange Curd (below)
1/2	cup vegetable oil		

Combine the flour, sugar, baking powder, baking soda and salt in a bowl and whisk to mix well. Combine the butter, oil, eggs, buttermilk, orange zest and lemon zest in a bowl and whisk until smooth.

Make a well in the center of the dry ingredients and add the liquid ingredients. Fold in gently with a rubber spatula, mixing just until moistened. Fold in the nuts. Do not overmix; the batter will be slightly lumpy.

Spray tiny dark nonstick muffin cups with nonstick cooking spray. Fill three-fourths full with the batter. Bake at 350 degrees for 15 to 20 minutes or until light brown. Serve with Orange Curd.

SERVES 12

Orange Curd

2/3	cup sugar	1/4	cup fresh lemon juice
2	tablespoons grated orange zest		Salt to taste
1	tablespoon grated lemon zest	1/4	cup (1/2 stick) unsalted
8	egg yolks		butter, chopped
1/2	cup fresh orange juice		

Combine the sugar, orange zest and lemon zest in a food processor or bowl. Process or mix with a fork until the sugar is colored and fragrant. Combine the sugar mixture with the egg yolks, orange juice and lemon juice in a saucepan. Cook over medium-high heat for 8 to 10 minutes or until the mixture thickens enough to coat the back of a spoon, whisking constantly. Remove from the heat.

Season with salt. Add the butter one piece at a time, stirring until smooth after each addition. Cover with plastic wrap, placing the wrap directly on the surface of the curd to prevent a skin from forming. Chill for 1 hour to 24 hours.

SERVES 12

Fennel and Coarse Salt Breadsticks

Jason Knapp, *Executive Chef of The Governor's Mansion*

2¹/2 teaspoons (¹/4 ounce) dry yeast
³/4   cup lukewarm water
1¹/2 teaspoons sugar
2¹/2 to 3 cups all-purpose flour
¹/4   cup olive oil
1   teaspoon table salt
      Cornmeal
1   egg
1   tablespoon water
      Fennel seeds to taste
      Coarse salt to taste

Combine the yeast with ³/4 cup lukewarm water and ¹/2 teaspoon of the sugar in a large mixing bowl; let stand for 5 minutes or until foamy. Add the remaining 1 teaspoon sugar, 2 cups of the flour, the olive oil and table salt and mix with a dough hook until smooth. Knead in enough of the remaining 1 cup flour to form a dough. Knead for 5 minutes or until soft but not sticky.

Cover with a kitchen towel on a lightly floured surface and let rest for 15 minutes. Divide the dough into twelve portions. Roll one portion at a time between the palms of the hands to form 14-inch ropes, leaving the remaining portions covered. Arrange the ropes 2 inches apart on baking sheets sprinkled lightly with cornmeal. Let rise, loosely covered, in a warm place for 40 minutes.

Whisk the egg with 1 tablespoon water in a bowl. Brush the egg wash over the ropes and sprinkle with fennel seeds and coarse salt. Bake at 450 degrees on the center oven rack for 12 to 15 minutes or until pale golden brown. Cool on a wire rack for 10 minutes. Store in an airtight container for up to 24 hours.

MAKES 12

Focaccia

2	tablespoons dry yeast	4³/4	cups bread flour
2	cups lukewarm water		Olive oil for brushing
5	teaspoons extra-virgin olive oil	1	tablespoon fresh thyme
2	teaspoons table salt	2	teaspoons fresh rosemary
1	tablespoon cracked pepper	2	teaspoons coarse sea salt

Mix the yeast with the water in a large bowl; let stand for several minutes. Add 5 teaspoons olive oil, the table salt and cracked pepper. Stir in 1 cup of the flour with a wooden spoon. Add the remaining flour 1/2 cup at a time, mixing until a soft but not sticky dough forms. Place in an oiled bowl, turning to coat the surface. Cover with plastic wrap and let rise in a warm place for 45 minutes; do not punch down the dough.

Remove gently to an oiled 10×15-inch baking sheet. Form dents in the dough with the index and middle fingers. Brush with additional olive oil and sprinkle with the thyme, rosemary and sea salt. Cover with plastic wrap and let rise in a warm place for 15 minutes. Bake at 450 degrees for 30 minutes.

SERVES 8

Oatmeal Bread

1	cup old-fashioned rolled oats	1/2	cup warm (100- to 110-degree)
2	cups boiling water		water
1/2	cup packed light brown sugar	1	tablespoon melted shortening
1	(1/4-ounce) envelope dry yeast	4¹/2	cups all-purpose flour

Stir the oats into the boiling water in a large bowl. Stir in the brown sugar; let stand until cool. Sprinkle the yeast over the warm water in a measuring cup. Stir until smooth. Add the shortening. Add to the oats mixture and stir in the flour. Cover with a kitchen towel and let rise in a warm draft-free place until doubled in bulk.

Punch down the dough and divide into two portions. Place each portion in a lightly greased 4×8-inch loaf pan. Let rise until doubled in bulk.

Bake at 350 degrees for 30 minutes or until the loaves test done. Slice and serve or toast. Do not substitute quick-cooking oats for the old-fashioned rolled oats.

MAKES 2 LOAVES

Snowed In

Tuscan White Bean Soup

51

Warm Cheese and Romaine Salad

72

Focaccia

196

Pecan Finger Pies

216

Wine: Vermentino

Cinnamon Rolls

ROLLS

1/2 cup shortening
1/2 cup sugar
1 cup boiling water
2 envelopes dry yeast
2 teaspoons sugar
1 cup warm water
2 eggs, beaten
1/2 cup (1 stick) butter, softened
6 cups (or more) all-purpose flour

1/2 teaspoon salt
3/4 cup sugar
2 tablespoons cinnamon
1/2 cup (1 stick) butter, melted

CONFECTIONERS' SUGAR GLAZE

1 cup confectioners' sugar
2 tablespoons milk
1/2 teaspoon vanilla extract

Combine the shortening and 1/2 cup sugar in a bowl and add the boiling water; mix to melt the shortening and dissolve the sugar. Let stand to cool.

Mix the yeast with 2 teaspoons sugar and the warm water in a bowl. Let stand for 10 to 15 minutes or until bubbly. Add to the shortening mixture. Add the eggs, softened butter, flour and salt. Mix well, adding additional flour if needed to form a soft and pliable but not sticky dough.

Place the dough in a greased bowl, turning to grease the surface. Cover with plastic wrap and a kitchen towel and let rise for 1 to 1 1/2 hours or until doubled in bulk. Punch down the dough and divide into two portions. Place the portions on a lightly floured surface and cover with plastic wrap. Let rest for 15 minutes.

Mix 3/4 cup sugar with the cinnamon in a cup. Roll one portion of the dough at a time into a rectangle 1/4 inch thick. Brush each portion with half the melted butter and sprinkle with half the cinnamon-sugar. Roll each from the long side to enclose the cinnamon-sugar. Cut into 1 1/4-inch slices.

Place the slices cut side down in lightly greased baking pans. Let rise in a warm place for 45 to 60 minutes. Bake at 400 degrees for 15 to 20 minutes or until light brown.

Mix the confectioners' sugar with the milk and vanilla in a bowl until of a glaze consistency. Spread over the cinnamon rolls. Serve warm.

SERVES 8

Refrigerator Rolls

$^1/_2$ cup sugar
1   teaspoon salt
2   cups lukewarm water
2   envelopes dry yeast
1   egg
5   cups all-purpose flour
$^1/_4$ cup shortening
   Melted butter for brushing

Stir the sugar and salt into the lukewarm water in a bowl. Add the yeast and stir until dissolved. Add the egg and beat until smooth. Add 2 cups of the flour and half the shortening; mix well. Add the remaining flour and shortening and mix to form a dough. Cover tightly and store in the refrigerator for several days.

Shape the dough into small balls and place three balls in each greased muffin cup. Let rise for 2 hours. Bake at 350 degrees for 20 minutes or until golden brown. Brush the tops with melted butter and serve hot.

MAKES 2 DOZEN

Monkey Bread

Thaw two one-pound loaves of frozen white bread dough. Combine one cup of sugar, one-fourth cup of brown sugar, and one and one-fourth teaspoons of cinnamon in a small saucepan. Bring the mixture to a boil and cook for 1 minute. Remove from the heat and cool for 10 minutes. Then combine one-fourth cup of sugar with one-half teaspoon of cinnamon in a shallow dish. Cut each loaf of bread dough into twenty-four equal portions. Roll each portion in the cinnamon-sugar and layer in a well-greased twelve-cup bundt pan. Pour the sugar syrup over the dough. Cover and let rise in a warm place until it has doubled in bulk. Uncover and bake at 350 degrees for 25 minutes. Loosen the edge with a knife and invert onto a serving platter.

Desserts

Savor the Sites

ARKANSAS ARTS CENTER

CARRIE REMMEL DICKINSON FOUNTAIN

The Junior League of Little Rock and the Fine Arts Club of Arkansas formed the core group of supporters and volunteers who helped create the Museum of Fine Art in Little Rock's MacArthur Park in 1937. Some twenty years later, in 1959, future governor Winthrop Rockefeller and his wife led a capital campaign to expand the museum. In 1960, the museum was renamed the Arkansas Arts Center to reflect the statewide focus of the institution. The Arkansas Arts Center's galleries showcase works from its internationally acclaimed permanent collection as well as a rich variety of special exhibitions. The permanent collection, focused on unique works on paper and contemporary objects in craft media, is highlighted by the world's largest collection of works by Paul Signac. The award-winning Children's Theatre and The Museum School offer inspiring opportunities to experience the arts, while The Artmobile, Traveling Exhibits, and Tell-a-Tale Troupe allow the entire state to enjoy the AAC's treasures. A museum shop specializing in original works and a restaurant offering global cuisine complete this destination for the best taste in art and entertainment.

Arkansas Blackberry Cake

CAKE
1   cup (2 sticks) butter, melted
1¹/2 cups sugar
4   eggs
1   cup blackberry jam
1   cup buttermilk
3   cups all-purpose flour
1   teaspoon baking soda

1   tablespoon cinnamon
1   tablespoon allspice
1   teaspoon ground cloves

JAM CAKE GLAZE
2   cups sugar
1   cup milk
1   teaspoon vanilla extract

Beat the butter and sugar in a mixing bowl until light and fluffy. Add the eggs one at a time, beating well after each addition. Beat in the jam and buttermilk. Add the flour, baking soda, cinnamon, allspice and cloves and beat until smooth. Spoon into two round 8-inch cake pans. Bake at 350 degrees for 1 hour or until a wooden pick inserted into the center comes out clean. Cool in the pans for several minutes. Remove to a wire rack to cool completely. Stack the layers on a cake plate.

Combine the sugar and milk in a medium saucepan. Cook to 234 to 240 degrees on a candy thermometer, soft-ball stage. Remove from the heat and stir in the vanilla. Beat until smooth. Spread between the layers and over the top and side of the cake.

SERVES 8

Museum of Discovery

Whether you are a child—or merely a child at heart—the Museum of Discovery will be an experience to remember. Established in 1927 as the Museum of Natural History and Antiquities, the Museum of Discovery is one of the oldest museums in Little Rock. This educational resource was first housed in City Hall and moved to the old Arsenal Building in MacArthur Park in 1942. In 1998, the museum moved to its current site in the River Market and was renamed Museum of Discovery. Prior to 1998, there was a League-wide shift requirement at the museum. The museum is now self-sustaining and is a Smithsonian Affiliate. JLLR underwrote the "Imagination Station" at the new site, where you can explore your creativity. Take a tour of the Bug Zoo. Whether for overnight camp-in, birthday party, or drop-by, the Museum of Discovery offers an exploration into science and nature.

Molten Chocolate Cakes with Orange Cranberry Cream

4	ounces semisweet chocolate	6	tablespoons all-purpose flour
1/2	cup (1 stick) butter	1	teaspoon Saigon cinnamon
1	tablespoon cabernet sauvignon	1	teaspoon ground ginger
1	cup confectioners' sugar, sifted	1/8	teaspoon ground cloves (optional)
1	teaspoon vanilla extract		Confectioners' sugar
2	eggs		Orange Cranberry Cream (below)
1	egg yolk		

*P*lace the chocolate and butter in a microwave-safe dish and microwave on High for 1 minute or until melted. Whisk to mix well. Stir in the wine, 1 cup confectioners' sugar and the vanilla. Whisk in the eggs and egg yolk. Stir in the flour, cinnamon, ginger and cloves.

Spoon into four buttered 6-ounce custard cups and place on a baking sheet. Bake at 425 degrees for 13 to 15 minutes or until the cakes are firm around the edge but soft in the center. Let stand for 1 minute. Loosen from the cups with a small knife and invert onto serving plates. Sprinkle with additional confectioners' sugar and top with Orange Cranberry Cream. Serve immediately.

You can also cover the unbaked cakes with plastic wrap and chill for up to 10 hours. Let stand at room temperature for 30 minutes before baking.

SERVES 4

Orange Cranberry Cream

1	cup heavy whipping cream	1	teaspoon orange extract
2	tablespoons confectioners' sugar	1	teaspoon vanilla extract
1	tablespoon jellied cranberry sauce		

*C*hill a large mixing bowl and whisk attachment. Combine the cream, confectioners' sugar, cranberry sauce, orange extract and vanilla in the chilled bowl. Beat at high speed until firm peaks form.

MAKES 2 CUPS

Decadent Flourless Chocolate Cake

9	ounces semisweet chocolate, chopped	1	tablespoon all-purpose flour
1/2	cup (1 stick) unsalted butter, softened	6	egg whites
3/4	cup granulated sugar		Pinch of cream of tartar
6	egg yolks		Pinch of salt
			Confectioners' sugar, for garnish

Butter the bottom and side of a 9-inch springform pan. Line the bottom with a circle of waxed paper and butter the paper. Coat with flour, shaking out the excess.

Melt the chocolate in a double boiler over simmering water, stirring constantly. Cream the butter and granulated sugar in a mixing bowl until light and fluffy. Add the melted chocolate and mix well. Beat in the egg yolks one at a time. Add the flour and mix until smooth. Chill, covered, just until firm. Beat the egg whites in a mixing bowl until foamy. Add the cream of tartar and salt and beat until soft peaks form. Fold one-third of the egg whites into the chocolate mixture. Fold in the remaining egg whites gently.

Spoon into the prepared springform pan. Bake at 450 degrees for 5 minutes. Reduce the oven temperature to 300 degrees and bake for 25 to 30 minutes longer or until a wooden pick inserted 2 inches from the outer edge comes out clean; the center will remain moist. Cool in the pan on a wire rack for 10 minutes. Invert onto a serving plate and remove the side and bottom of the pan. Cool completely and garnish with confectioners' sugar.

SERVES 10

Coconut Cake

2	(2-layer) packages moist white cake mix	1	cup sour cream
12	ounces sweetened whipped topping	1	(14-ounce) package flaked coconut
2	cups sugar	1	(15-ounce) can cream of coconut

Prepare and bake the cake mix in four 8-inch round cake pans, using the package directions. Cool in the pans for 5 to 10 minutes. Remove to wire racks to cool completely. Combine the whipped topping, sugar and sour cream in a bowl. Reserve 1 cup of the coconut and fold the remaining coconut into the whipped topping mixture. Chill in the refrigerator.

Cut off the rounded tops of the cake layers to make them flat. Place one layer on a cake plate and drizzle with one-third of the cream of coconut. Frost the top and side of the layer with 1 cup of the whipped topping mixture. Repeat with the remaining layers and whipped topping mixture.

Sprinkle 1/4 cup of the reserved coconut on top of the cake and press the remaining reserved coconut onto the side. Chill for 24 hours or longer before serving.

SERVES 12

Lemon Cream Cake

CRUMB TOPPING

1/2 cup all-purpose flour

1/2 cup confectioners' sugar

1/2 teaspoon vanilla extract

1/4 cup (1/2 stick) butter, chilled and chopped

CAKE

1 (2-layer) package white cake mix

1 1/4 cups water

1/3 cup vegetable oil

3 egg whites

Lemon Cream (below)

Confectioners sugar, for garnish

*M*ix the flour and confectioners' sugar in a medium bowl. Drizzle with the vanilla and add the butter. Mix with the hands to the consistency of crumbs; do not press the mixture together.

*C*ombine the cake mix, water, oil and egg whites in a bowl and prepare using the cake mix directions. Spoon into a greased 10-inch cake pan or springform pan. Bake at 350 degrees for 40 to 45 minutes or until the cake tests done. Cool in the pan for several minutes. Remove to a wire rack to cool completely.

Cut the cake into halves horizontally. Place the bottom half on a cake plate. Spread with 1/2 cup of the Lemon Cream. Replace the top half and spread the remaining Lemon Cream over the top and side of the cake. Sprinkle the crumb topping over the top of the cake and press over the side.

Chill for 3 hours or longer. Cut into 12 slices and garnish the slices with confectioners' sugar.

SERVES 12

Lemon Cream

8 ounces cream cheese, softened

2 cups confectioners' sugar

4 teaspoons lemon juice

1 cup heavy whipping cream

*B*eat the cream cheese and confectioners' sugar in a large mixing bowl until smooth. Mix in the lemon juice. Whip the cream at high speed in a mixing bowl until firm peaks form. Fold into the cream cheese mixture.

SERVES 12

Mocha Bundt Cake

1   (2-layer) package devil's food cake mix
1   small package chocolate instant pudding mix
4   eggs
1   cup sour cream
1/2   cup vegetable oil
1/2   cup cold coffee
2   cups (12 ounces) chocolate chips
1   cup confectioners' sugar
2   tablespoons strong coffee
2   tablespoons Kahlúa
2   tablespoons crème de cacao

Combine the cake mix, pudding mix, eggs, sour cream, oil and 1/2 cup coffee in a bowl and mix until smooth. Fold in the chocolate chips. Spoon into a greased 10-inch bundt pan. Bake at 350 degrees for 50 minutes. Punch holes in the warm cake.

Combine the confectioners' sugar, 2 tablespoons coffee, the liqueur and crème de cacao in a bowl; mix well. Drizzle over the cake. Let stand until cool and invert onto a serving plate.

SERVES 12

River Rail System

All aboard! When visiting downtown Little Rock, take a ride on the River Rail System. It is a replica of the streetcar trolleys of old. Passengers are delighted by the view of the Arkansas River and the downtown skyline. Travel between the River Market district and North Little Rock, stopping at Alltel Arena, the Statehouse Convention Center, Riverfront Park, Historic Arkansas Museum, Robinson Auditorium Concert Hall, Museum of Discovery, and unique shops, art galleries, libraries, and restaurants. When downtown, it's the way to travel!

Strawberry Layer Cake

1   *(2-layer) package yellow butter cake mix*
2/3 cup canola oil
1   *(4-ounce) package strawberry gelatin*
4   *eggs*
1   *cup thawed frozen strawberries, coarsely chopped*
1   *teaspoon vanilla extract*
1/2 cup strawberry jam
      Strawberry Frosting (below)
12   *fresh strawberries, sliced lengthwise, for garnish*

*L*ine the bottoms of three round 9-inch cake pans with circles of baking parchment and spray the parchment with nonstick cooking spray. Combine the cake mix, canola oil and gelatin in a mixing bowl and mix well. Beat in the eggs one at a time. Add the strawberries and vanilla and mix until smooth. Spoon into the prepared cake pans.

Bake at 300 degrees for 25 to 30 minutes or until a wooden pick inserted into the center comes out clean. Cool in the pans on a wire rack.

Loosen the layers from the pans with a knife. Place one layer on a cake plate and spread with 1/4 cup of the strawberry jam. Add the second layer and spread with the remaining 1/4 cup jam. Top with the third layer and spread the Strawberry Frosting over the top and side of the cake. Garnish with the fresh strawberries arranged to cover the top of the cake.

SERVES 8 TO 10

Strawberry Frosting

4   *ounces cream cheese, softened*
2   *tablespoons butter, softened*
1   *(1-pound) package confectioners' sugar*
1/3 cup (or more) thawed frozen strawberries,
      coarsely chopped

*C*ombine the cream cheese, butter, confectioners' sugar and strawberries in a bowl and mix until of spreading consistency. Add 1 teaspoon additional strawberries if the frosting is too stiff.

FROSTS 1 (3-LAYER) CAKE

Island Key Lime Torte

Key Lime Filling

2 *cups whipping cream*
1 *(14-ounce) can sweetened condensed milk*
3 *tablespoons lemon juice*
3 *tablespoons Key lime juice*
2 *teaspoons grated Key lime zest*

Torte

3/4 *cup plus 2 tablespoons butter, softened*
3/4 *cup confectioners' sugar*
1¹/4 *cups all-purpose flour*
2 *tablespoons yellow cornmeal*
1/2 *cup chopped macadamia nuts*
1/2 *cup sweetened flaked coconut*
1 *(12-ounce) jar lemon curd*
1/4 *cup coconut, toasted*
   Thin lime slices

Whip the cream in a mixing bowl until firm peaks form. Combine the condensed milk, lemon juice, lime juice and lime zest in a medium bowl. Fold in 2 cups of the whipped cream. Reserve the remaining whipped cream for the assembly.

Cream the butter and confectioners' sugar in a mixing bowl until light and fluffy. Add the flour and cornmeal and mix well. Stir in the macadamia nuts and 1/2 cup coconut. Divide the dough into halves and press each half into an 8-inch circle on an ungreased baking sheet. Bake at 325 degrees for 20 minutes. Cool on the baking sheets for 10 minutes. Remove to a wire rack to cool completely.

Place one cooled shortbread round on a serving plate. Spread gently with half the lemon curd. Top with half the Key lime filling. Spread the remaining lemon curd on the second shortbread round and place on the first. Spread with the remaining Key lime filling.

Spread the reserved whipped cream over the top and sprinkle with the lime zest and toasted coconut. Chill, covered, for several hours before serving. Garnish with lime slices.

Serves 12

Pinnacle Mountain Picnic

Peperonata

21

Spicy Pimento Cheese Sandwiches

23

German Potato Salad

73

Grilled Fruit Kabobs

177

Carrot Cupcakes with Cream Cheese Icing

211

Wine: Viognier

Carrot Cupcakes with Cream Cheese Icing

CUPCAKES

2 cups all-purpose flour
2 teaspoons baking soda
2 teaspoons cinnamon
1/2 teaspoon salt
3 eggs
2 cups granulated sugar
1/4 cup packed brown sugar
3/4 cup vegetable oil
1 1/2 cups buttermilk
1 tablespoon vanilla extract
2 cups finely grated carrots

1 (8-ounce) can crushed
  pineapple, drained
1 (3-ounce) can sweetened
  flaked coconut
1 cup chopped pecans

CREAM CHEESE ICING

1/2 cup (1 stick) butter, softened
12 ounces cream cheese, softened
2 cups confectioners' sugar
1 teaspoon vanilla extract

Mix the flour, baking soda, cinnamon and salt together. Beat the eggs in a large bowl. Add the granulated sugar, brown sugar, oil, buttermilk and vanilla and mix until smooth. Add the flour mixture gradually, beating at low speed until blended. Fold in the carrots, pineapple, coconut and pecans.

Spoon into paper-lined muffin cups. Bake at 350 degrees for 25 minutes. Remove to a wire rack to cool.

Cream the butter and cream cheese in a mixing bowl until light. Add the confectioners' sugar and vanilla and beat until fluffy. Spread over the tops of the cupcakes.

MAKES 30

Almond-Filled Cupcakes

1   (12-ounce) can almond cake and pastry filling
1   egg
1   cup (6 ounces) dark chocolate chips
1¹/2 cups all-purpose flour
3/4 cup sugar
1/4 cup baking cocoa
1   teaspoon baking soda
1/2 teaspoon salt
1   cup water
2   tablespoons vegetable oil
1   tablespoon white vinegar
1   teaspoon almond extract
1   cup sliced almonds

Combine the cake and pastry filling with the egg in a small bowl and mix well. Stir in the chocolate chips.

Mix the flour, sugar, baking cocoa, baking soda and salt in a mixing bowl. Add the water, oil, vinegar and almond extract and mix well. Spoon into greased or paper-lined muffin cups, filling one-third full.

Spoon 1 teaspoon of the almond filling mixture into each muffin cup and sprinkle with the almonds. Bake at 350 degrees for 20 to 24 minutes or until golden brown.

MAKES 20 TO 24

The Little Rock Zoo

If it's animals and family fun you like, then the zoo is for you! In 1926, the Little Rock Zoo opened with only a trained circus bear and an abandoned timber wolf. Today, it's home to 750 animals representing more than two hundred different species, many of which are endangered. Located on thirty-three acres in War Memorial Park in the heart of Little Rock's midtown neighborhood, the zoo is one of Arkansas's greatest treasures and features the Over-the-Jumps Carousel, a fully restored antique carousel that is the only one of its kind in operation. Wild and wonderful.

Fudge Brownies

1¹/2 cups all-purpose flour
¹/2 teaspoon baking soda
¹/2 teaspoon salt
1¹/2 cups sugar
¹/3 cup Kahlúa
6 tablespoons butter

2 cups (12 ounces) dark
   chocolate chips
2 teaspoons almond extract
3 eggs
1 cup sliced almonds

Mix the flour with the baking soda and salt. Combine the sugar, liqueur and butter in a large microwave-safe bowl. Microwave on High for 2 minutes or until the butter melts; stir until smooth. Add the chocolate chips and almond extract and mix by hand. Beat in the eggs one at a time at low speed. Add the flour mixture gradually, mixing well after each addition.

Spoon into a greased baking dish. Sprinkle with the almonds. Bake at 325 degrees for 30 to 35 minutes or until set. You can also bake in a metal baking pan at 350 degrees.

SERVES 12

Green Apple Squares

1 (2-layer) package yellow cake mix
¹/2 cup (1 stick) butter, softened
¹/2 cup flaked coconut
1¹/2 cups thinly sliced green apples

¹/3 cup sugar
1 teaspoon cinnamon
1 cup sour cream
1 egg, beaten

Combine the cake mix, butter and coconut in a bowl and mix well. Press the mixture into a greased 9×13-inch baking pan, pressing slightly up the sides. Bake at 350 degrees for 10 minutes.

Arrange the apple slices over the baked layer and sprinkle with the sugar and cinnamon. Blend the sour cream and egg in a small bowl. Drizzle over the apples. Bake for 25 minutes longer; do not overbake.

MAKES 12 TO 15

Chocolate Peanut Butter Squares

1/4	cup packed dark brown sugar	2	(4-ounce) milk chocolate bars
1 1/2	cups confectioners' sugar	1	(4-ounce) semisweet chocolate bar
2	cups creamy peanut butter	2	tablespoons unsalted butter

Combine the brown sugar, confectioners' sugar and peanut butter in a bowl and beat with a hand mixer; some of the brown sugar lumps may remain. Press into a greased 9×9-inch pan.

Combine the milk chocolate, semisweet chocolate and butter in a microwave-safe bowl. Microwave on Medium for 1 to 2 minutes or until melted; mix well. Spread over the peanut butter layer. Chill until set. Cut into small squares to serve.

SERVES 12

Cinnamon Crisp Bars

1	cup (2 sticks) butter, softened	2	teaspoons cinnamon
1	cup sugar		Pinch of salt
1	egg yolk	1	egg white, lightly beaten
2	cups all-purpose flour	2	cups chopped pecans

Beat the butter and sugar in a mixing bowl until light and fluffy. Add the egg yolk, flour, cinnamon and salt and mix well. Press over an ungreased baking sheet or jelly roll pan with sides, pressing with the bottom of a glass to spread evenly; the layer will be very thin.

Brush with the egg white and sprinkle with the pecans. Bake at 325 degrees for 30 to 35 minutes or until the center is firm. Cool on a wire rack and cut into bars.

MAKES 21

War Memorial Stadium

War Memorial Stadium, dedicated in 1948 as a memorial to the veterans of the First and Second World Wars, is an Arkansas landmark where some of the state's most significant sports memories have been made. With a seating capacity of nearly 54,000, War Memorial is best known as the second home to the University of Arkansas Razorback football team, and that's just the kickoff. Other major colleges and universities schedule games periodically at War Memorial, and it is where you'll find the State High School Football Championships. However, War Memorial is more than sports. It's where concerts, religious presentations, military celebrations, sales, and birthday parties take place. War Memorial Stadium is definitely a site for competition and celebration!

Cupboard Cookies

1/2	cup (1 stick) butter, softened	1	cup all-purpose flour
1/2	cup granulated sugar	1/2	cup rolled oats
1/3	cup packed brown sugar	1	teaspoon baking soda
1/2	cup peanut butter	1/4	teaspoon salt
1	egg	1	cup (6 ounces) chocolate chips
1/2	teaspoon vanilla extract	1	cup (6 ounces) peanut butter chips

Combine the butter, granulated sugar, brown sugar, peanut butter, egg and vanilla in a mixing bowl and beat until creamy. Add the flour, oats, baking soda and salt; mix well. Stir in the chocolate chips and peanut butter chips.

Drop by spoonfuls onto a nonstick cookie sheet. Bake at 350 degrees for 10 to 12 minutes or until golden brown. Cool on the cookie sheet for several minutes. Remove to a wire rack to cool completely.

MAKES 2 DOZEN

Cream Cheese Cookies

1	cup (2 sticks) butter, softened	2	cups all-purpose flour
1	cup sugar	1 1/2	teaspoons vanilla extract
3	ounces cream cheese, softened	1	cup finely chopped pecans

Process the butter, sugar, cream cheese, flour and vanilla in a food processor until smooth. Fold in the pecans. Shape into two rolls and wrap in plastic wrap. Chill for several hours or until firm.

Cut the rolls into thin slices. Arrange on a greased cookie sheet. Bake at 350 degrees for 8 to 10 minutes or until light golden brown.

SERVES 12

Pecan Finger Pies

Irene Wassell, *Food Editor,* Arkansas Democrat-Gazette

CRUMB CRUST
1¹/4 cups all-purpose flour
¹/3 cup sugar
¹/2 cup (1 stick) butter

FINGER PIES
²/3 cup sugar
³/4 cup honey
2 eggs
2 tablespoons all-purpose flour
2 tablespoons butter, melted
¹/4 teaspoon vanilla extract
1 cup chopped pecans

Combine the flour, sugar and butter in a 1-quart mixing bowl and beat at low speed for 30 to 60 seconds to form coarse crumbs, scraping the side of the bowl frequently. Press into a 9×9-inch or 7×11-inch baking pan. Bake at 350 degrees on the center oven rack for 10 to 15 minutes or until the edges are light brown.

Place the sugar, honey, eggs, flour, melted butter and vanilla in a 1-quart mixing bowl. Beat at low speed for 1 to 2 minutes or until smooth. Stir in the pecans. Spread evenly over the crust. Bake for 20 to 25 minutes or until the filling is golden brown and set in the center. Cool on a wire rack. Cut into bars.

MAKES 2 DOZEN

Nearby Nature

Located in the heart of the Natural State, Little Rock puts nature up close and personal nearly every way you turn. With more than fifty parks, our city offers a wide array of outdoor fun, from hiking to golf to tennis to playgrounds in historic sites, to name a few. An exciting day trip awaits at Pinnacle Mountain State Park on the city's western border, with a mountain climb, forty miles of hiking trails, picnic areas, and the Arkansas Arboretum. And if your spirit of outdoor adventure includes hunting, fishing, and boating, then we've got you covered in all four seasons with Arkansas's first-class state park system and a wide variety of lakes and rivers. Go green…go Arkansas!

Pumpkin Cookies

COOKIES
1   cup shortening
1   cup sugar
1 3/4 cups all-purpose flour
1   teaspoon baking powder
1   teaspoon baking soda
2   teaspoons cinnamon
1   teaspoon allspice
1/2   teaspoon salt
1   egg
1   cup pumpkin
1/2   cup chopped nuts (optional)
1   teaspoon vanilla extract

BROWN SUGAR FROSTING
1   cup packed brown sugar
3   tablespoons margarine
1/4   cup milk
1   cup confectioners' sugar
1   teaspoon vanilla extract

Cream the shortening and sugar in a mixing bowl until light and fluffy. Add the flour, baking powder, baking soda, cinnamon, allspice and salt; mix until smooth. Mix in the egg, pumpkin, nuts and vanilla.

Drop by small spoonfuls onto a lightly greased cookie sheet. Bake at 350 degrees for 8 to 10 minutes or until golden brown.

Bring the brown sugar, margarine and milk just to a boil in a saucepan, stirring to mix well. Cool for 1 hour or longer. Stir in the confectioners' sugar and vanilla. Spread over the cookies and let stand for 1 to 2 hours or until the frosting is set.

MAKES 2 DOZEN

Iced Sugar Cookies

COOKIES

3	cups all-purpose flour
1	teaspoon baking soda
1/2	teaspoon salt
1	cup (2 sticks) butter, softened
1	cup sugar
2	eggs
2	teaspoons vanilla extract

CONFECTIONERS' SUGAR ICING

1	cup confectioners' sugar
2	tablespoons milk
1	teaspoon vanilla extract
	Several drops of food coloring

Whisk the flour, baking soda and salt together in a medium bowl. Cream the butter and sugar in a mixing bowl until light and fluffy. Beat in the eggs and vanilla. Add the flour mixture gradually, beating at low speed to form a dough.

Divide the dough into three portions and shape each portion into a disk. Wrap in plastic wrap. Chill for 2 to 12 hours.

Roll one portion at a time 1/8 inch thick on a lightly floured surface, leaving the other portions in the refrigerator. Cut into desired shapes and arrange 2 inches apart on ungreased cookie sheets. Bake at 350 degrees for 10 minutes or until the edges begin to brown. Cool on wire racks.

Combine the confectioners' sugar, milk and vanilla in a mixing bowl and mix until smooth. Tint as desired. Spread or pipe on the cookies. You can use holiday cookie cutters or other cutters to suit the season for these cookies.

MAKES 3 1/2 DOZEN

Cookie Tips

Cold cookie dough is essential for success when rolling out cookies to cut. Work with small amounts of dough at a time and keep the rest in the refrigerator until ready to use.
When decorating cookies, thicken the icing with additional confectioners' sugar for use in detail work. Spoon the icing into a sealable plastic bag, cut one corner, and pipe the icing in the desired design onto the cookies. Let the cookies stand for several hours to allow the icing to set before serving.

Éclair Pie

3	cups heavy whipping cream	2	envelopes premelted chocolate
1	(1-pound) package		(tested with Nestlé)
	confectioners' sugar	3	tablespoons margarine,
2	small packages French vanilla		partially melted
	instant pudding mix	1¹/2	cups confectioners' sugar, sifted
3¹/2	cups milk	3	tablespoons milk
1	baked pie shell	2	tablespoons light corn syrup

*C*ombine the cream and 1 pound confectioners' sugar in a mixing bowl and beat until light and fluffy. Combine the pudding mix with 3¹/2 cups milk in a mixing bowl and beat for 2 minutes. Blend in half the whipped cream mixture. Spoon into the pie shell. Chill for 2 hours.

Combine the chocolate, margarine, 1¹/2 cups confectioners' sugar, 3 tablespoons milk and the corn syrup in a mixing bowl; beat until smooth. Spread over the pie. Top with the remaining whipped cream mixture.

SERVES 8

Peanut Butter Pie

CHOCOLATE PEANUT CRUST		PIE	
1	cup chopped dry-roasted peanuts	8	ounces cream cheese, softened
1	cup graham cracker crumbs	1	cup crunchy peanut butter
¹/4	cup (¹/2 stick) butter, melted	1	cup confectioners' sugar
¹/4	cup sugar	1¹/2	cups heavy whipping cream
¹/3	cup shaved semisweet chocolate	¹/4	cup granulated sugar
			Chopped peanuts and shaved
			chocolate, for garnish

*M*ix the peanuts, graham cracker crumbs, butter and sugar in a bowl. Press over the bottom and up the side of a pie plate. Bake at 350 degrees for 10 minutes or until golden brown and set. Remove from the oven and sprinkle the shaved chocolate over the bottom immediately.

*C*ombine the cream cheese, peanut butter and confectioners' sugar in a mixing bowl and beat until smooth. Combine the cream and granulated sugar in a mixing bowl and beat until soft peaks form. Fold into the peanut butter mixture. Spoon into the prepared crust. Chill for several hours before serving. Garnish with additional peanuts and shaved chocolate.

SERVES 8

Pumpkin Chiffon Pie

3   egg yolks
1/2   cup sugar
11/4   cups canned or cooked fresh pumpkin
1/2   cup milk
1/2   teaspoon ginger
1/2   teaspoon nutmeg
1/2   teaspoon cinnamon
1/2   teaspoon salt
1   tablespoon unflavored gelatin
1/4   cup water
3   egg whites
1/2   cup sugar
1/4   cup pecans, chopped
1   pie shell
       Whipped cream, for garnish

Beat the egg yolks with 1/2 cup sugar in a mixing bowl. Combine with the pumpkin, milk, ginger, nutmeg, cinnamon and salt in a double boiler over simmering water and mix well. Cook until thickened, stirring constantly. Sprinkle the gelatin over the water in a cup. Let stand for 3 to 5 minutes or until softened. Add to the pumpkin mixture and stir until completely dissolved. Cool until thickened.

Beat the egg whites in a mixing bowl until soft peaks form. Add 1/2 cup sugar and beat until stiff peaks form. Fold into the pumpkin mixture. Sprinkle the pecans in the pie shell and bake using the package directions. Spoon the pumpkin mixture into the pie shell. Store in the refrigerator. Garnish with whipped cream.

SERVES 6 TO 8

Raspberry Brie Cheesecake Pie

2   cups sour cream
4   ounces cream cheese, softened
16   ounces Brie cheese, thinly sliced
1¹/2   cups sugar
2   eggs, beaten
12   ounces fresh raspberries
1   graham cracker pie shell

*C*ombine the sour cream, cream cheese, Brie cheese, sugar and eggs in a saucepan. Cook over low heat until the Brie and cream cheese melt. Remove from the heat and beat until smooth. Fold in three-fourths of the raspberries.

Spoon into the pie shell. Bake at 400 degrees for 25 minutes. Cool to room temperature. Chill in the refrigerator. Top with the remaining raspberries and serve chilled.

SERVES 8

Big Dam Bridge

Opened in 2007, the Big Dam Bridge—more than four thousand feet long—is the longest bicycle and pedestrian bridge ever built. The structure spans the Arkansas River, which is a part of the inland waterway system known as the McClellan-Kerr Navigation System, originating at the Tulsa Port in Oklahoma and running southeast to the Mississippi River. Friends and family from both sides of the river can cross only on two feet or two wheels. This site is unique in that it is the only bridge that has been built into a dam, providing a spectacular sight and a healthy incentive for viewing.

Cherry Cookie Cobblers

1   (16-ounce) package frozen dark sweet pitted cherries
1/4 cup (1/2 stick) butter
1/2 cup packed brown sugar
1/2 teaspoon cinnamon
1   teaspoon cornstarch
1   tablespoon water
1   roll refrigerator sugar cookie dough
     Granulated sugar for sprinkling
     Pecan pieces

Combine the cherries, butter, brown sugar and cinnamon in a saucepan. Bring to a boil and reduce the heat. Simmer for 20 minutes. Blend the cornstarch and water in a small bowl. Add to the cherries and cook for 3 to 5 minutes or until thickened, stirring constantly.

Spoon into four 7-ounce custard cups. Cut the cookie dough into twelve 1/4-inch slices. Place three slices on the top of each custard cup. Sprinkle with granulated sugar and pecans. Place on a large baking sheet. Bake at 350 degrees for 20 to 25 minutes or until the cookie topping is golden brown. Serve with a scoop of vanilla ice cream, if desired.

SERVES 4

Little Rock Memories

"One of my favorite Little Rock memories is a recent memory. I was honored to be with Ruth Lincoln as she celebrated her 110th birthday in the middle of the Big Dam Bridge over the Arkansas River. Born in 1897, Ruth chose as this year's adventure seeing the spectacular views, up toward Pinnacle Mountain and down toward the Clinton Presidential Library, from the highest point of one of Central Arkansas' newest structures, a bike and pedestrian bridge which will create memories for all of us for years to come."

—Vic Snyder
United States Congressman

Rustic Pear Tart

^{1}/3   cup all-purpose flour
^{1}/3   cup packed brown sugar
^{1}/4   teaspoon cinnamon
1   tablespoon finely chopped crystallized ginger
^{1}/4   cup chopped hazelnuts
4   Anjou pears, cut into ^{1}/8-inch slices
2   tablespoons fresh lemon juice
1   refrigerator pie pastry
2   tablespoons yellow cornmeal
1   tablespoon butter, chilled and finely chopped
1 or 2 tablespoons honey, slightly warmed
        Heavy cream for brushing
        Granulated sugar for sprinkling
        Whipped cream, for garnish

Mix the flour, brown sugar, cinnamon, ginger and hazelnuts in a bowl. Add the pears and lemon juice and toss to coat well.

Cut a 10-inch circle from baking parchment and place on a baking sheet with no sides. Roll the pie pastry into a 14-inch circle on a surface sprinkled with the cornmeal. Fold the pastry into quarters and place on the parchment; unfold.

Spoon the pear mixture onto the pastry, leaving a 2-inch edge. Dot with the butter and drizzle with the honey. Pull the pastry edge up and pleat over the filling. Brush the edge with cream and sprinkle with granulated sugar.

Bake at 400 degrees for 35 to 40 minutes or until golden brown. Cut into wedges and serve warm. Garnish with whipped cream.

SERVES 8

Chocolate Raspberry Truffle Torte

Paul Novicky, *Chef*

1/2	cup (1 stick) butter, softened	1	cup heavy cream
1/2	cup sugar	12	ounces bittersweet
3/4	teaspoon vanilla extract		chocolate, chopped
	Salt to taste	1	teaspoon butter
1	cup all-purpose flour	1	cup seedless raspberry preserves
1/3	cup baking cocoa		

Beat 1/2 cup butter with the sugar, vanilla and salt in a mixing bowl until light and fluffy. Add the flour and baking cocoa and mix well. Shape into a ball and wrap in plastic wrap. Chill for 1 hour.

Roll the dough 1/8 inch thick on a lightly floured surface. Fit into a tart pan and trim; prick the surface with a fork. Bake at 350 degrees for 15 minutes or until set. Cool to room temperature on a wire rack.

Bring the cream just to a boil in a saucepan. Pour over the chocolate and 1 teaspoon butter in a mixing bowl. Let stand for 5 minutes to melt the chocolate and butter. Whisk until smooth. Stir in the preserves. Spoon into the tart shell and chill for 2 hours or longer.

SERVES 10

Grasshopper Tartlets

22	chocolate sandwich cookies	2	cups heavy cream
	(tested with Oreos)	1/4	cup crème de menthe
1/4	cup (1/2 stick) butter, melted	1	(7-ounce) jar marshmallow creme

Crush the cookies with a rolling pin or process in a food processor. Combine with the melted butter in a bowl and mix well. Line thirty-six 2-inch muffin cups with foil or paper liners. Place 1 heaping teaspoon of the crumb mixture in each muffin cup and tamp down with a pastry tamper or the bottom of a small container, such as a film canister. Reserve the remaining crumbs.

Combine the cream and crème de menthe in a large mixing bowl. Beat at high speed until very soft peaks form. Add the marshmallow creme in large dollops, beating constantly until the mixture begins to thicken but is not dry. Spoon or pipe the mixture into the prepared muffin cups. Sprinkle with the reserved crumb mixture.

Freeze the tartlets until firm. Serve immediately or remove to an airtight container and freeze for up to 2 weeks.

For Brandy Alexander Tartlets, substitute 3 tablespoons brandy and 3 tablespoons crème de cacao for the crème de menthe.

MAKES 36

Frozen Cappuccino Cheesecake with Chocolate Sauce

CASHEW CRUST
1 cup cashews
1 cup chocolate cookie crumbs
3 tablespoons sugar
$^1/_3$ cup butter, melted

CHEESECAKE
1 cup heavy whipping cream
2 cups (12 ounces) semisweet
   chocolate chips
1 teaspoon vanilla extract

$^1/_2$ teaspoon salt
2 tablespoons espresso or very
   strong coffee
2 cups confectioners' sugar
24 ounces cream cheese, softened
1 cup heavy whipping cream
   Chocolate Sauce (below) or
   raspberry sauce
   Fresh raspberries, for garnish
   Sprigs of mint, for garnish

Process the cashews in a food processor until chopped. Add the cookie crumbs, sugar and melted butter and pulse just until mixed. Press into a lightly greased springform pan. Bake at 350 degrees for 10 to 12 minutes or until light brown. Cool to room temperature.

Bring 1 cup cream to a boil in a saucepan. Pour over the chocolate chips, vanilla and salt in a bowl and stir until smooth. Stir in the espresso. Cream the confectioners' sugar with the cream cheese in a mixing bowl until light and fluffy. Beat in the chocolate mixture.

Beat 1 cup cream in a mixing bowl until firm peaks form. Fold into the chocolate mixture. Spoon into the crust. Freeze until firm. Let stand at room temperature for 20 minutes. Loosen from the side of the springform pan and remove the side. Cut into wedges and place on serving plates. Drizzle with the Chocolate Sauce to serve. Garnish with raspberries and sprigs of mint.

SERVES 12

Chocolate Sauce

2 squares German's sweet
   chocolate
2 squares bittersweet chocolate

$^1/_2$ cup sugar
$^1/_2$ cup heavy cream

Combine the German's sweet chocolate, bittersweet chocolate, sugar and $^1/4$ cup of the cream in a double boiler. Cook over simmering water until thickened, stirring to blend well and adding as much of the remaining $^1/4$ cup cream as needed for the desired consistency.

MAKES 1 CUP

Praline Cheesecake

PECAN CRUST
1   cup graham cracker crumbs
1/4 cup finely chopped pecans
1/3 cup butter, softened
3   tablespoons sugar

CHEESECAKE
24   ounces cream cheese, softened
1   cup packed brown sugar
3   eggs
2   teaspoons vanilla extract
     Praline Sauce (below)

Combine the graham cracker crumbs, pecans, butter and sugar in a bowl and mix well. Press over the bottom and 1 inch up the side of a greased 9-inch springform pan. Bake at 350 degrees for 8 minutes. Reduce the oven temperature to 325 degrees.

Beat the cream cheese in a mixing bowl until smooth. Add the brown sugar and mix well. Beat in the eggs one at a time. Stir in the vanilla. Spoon into the prepared springform pan. Bake at 325 degrees for 40 minutes. Turn off the oven and let stand in the oven with the door ajar for 30 minutes. Cool to room temperature. Chill, covered, for 8 hours or longer.

Place on a serving plate and remove the side of the pan. Cut into wedges and serve with the warm Praline Sauce.

SERVES 8

Praline Sauce

2   tablespoons brown sugar
2   tablespoons cornstarch
1   cup dark corn syrup

1/2 cup coarsely chopped pecans
1   teaspoon vanilla extract

Mix the brown sugar and cornstarch in a small heavy saucepan. Add the corn syrup and mix well. Cook over medium heat until thickened, stirring constantly. Remove from the heat and stir in the pecans and vanilla. Serve warm.

MAKES 1³/4 CUPS

Creamy Praline Sauce

Melt one stick of butter in a medium saucepan. Stir in one and one-half cups of packed brown sugar and two tablespoons of light corn syrup. Add one-half cup of heavy cream and return to a boil. Remove from the heat and stir in one-fourth cup of chopped pecans. Serve warm over cheesecake, cake, or ice cream. Store in the refrigerator. Makes 2 cups.

Apple Raisin Compote

3	Granny Smith apples, chopped	1/2	cup brandy
3/4	cup raisins	1/2	cup walnuts, chopped
3/4	cup packed light brown sugar		

Combine the apples, raisins, brown sugar, brandy and walnuts in a medium saucepan. Cook, covered, over medium heat until the apples are tender and the brown sugar dissolves, stirring occasionally. Serve as a compote or over vanilla ice cream.

SERVES 4

Peaches and Basil

8   fresh peaches
3   tablespoons lime juice
1   cup peach schnapps
1/4   cup julienned fresh basil

Peel and slice the peaches. Combine with the lime juice, schnapps and basil in a bowl; mix gently. Chill in the refrigerator to blend the flavors. Serve in martini glasses.

SERVES 8

Apple Raisin Compote

Apple Raisin Compote is a versatile dish that can be presented in several different ways other than as a dessert. Consider pairing it with cheese for an appetizer course, serving it as an accompaniment, or assembling it on crostini. It can also be served during the main course as a tasty side dish of fruit or a chunky sauce over pork or chicken.

Strawberry Meringue Cups

2   egg whites
$^1/4$ teaspoon cream of tartar
$^1/2$ cup granulated sugar
2   cartons strawberries, sliced
1   cup granulated sugar
3   tablespoons Grand Marnier (optional)
2   cups heavy whipping cream
1   cup sifted confectioners' sugar

Beat the egg whites with the cream of tartar in a mixing bowl until foamy. Beat in $^1/2$ cup granulated sugar 1 tablespoon at a time, beating until stiff and glossy; do not underbeat.

Spoon into greased muffin cups and press gently against the bottom and side of each cup to form a cup. Bake at 275 degrees for 45 minutes. Turn off the oven and let stand in the closed oven for 45 minutes longer. Cool in a draft-free place.

Combine the strawberries with 1 cup granulated sugar and the liqueur in a bowl. Beat the cream with the confectioners' sugar in a mixing bowl until soft peaks form.

Remove the meringue cups to serving plates. Fill with the strawberry mixture and top with the whipped cream.

SERVES 8

Angel Pie is another great way to wow your guests with meringue. Make the meringue according to the directions in the Strawberry Meringue Cups recipe above, spreading it in a greased pie pan instead of muffin cups. After baking and cooling it, fill the pie crust with your favorite ice cream and chill in the freezer. Let stand at room temperature for 10 minutes before serving. Top with caramel sauce or chocolate sauce.

Almond Peach Trifle

CUSTARD
1   (14-ounce) can sweetened condensed milk
1/2 cup water
1/4 cup cornstarch
2   eggs
3   cups milk
1/2 cup (1 stick) butter
1   teaspoon vanilla extract
1   teaspoon almond extract

TRIFLE
1/4 cup sugar
8   large fresh peaches, peeled and sliced
1   pound cake, cut into 1/2-inch slices
1/2 cup amaretto
1   cup whipped cream
1/2 cup toasted sliced almonds

Combine the condensed milk, water, cornstarch and eggs in a bowl and mix until smooth. Combine the milk and butter in a saucepan and heat until the butter melts. Add the egg mixture gradually and cook over low heat for 20 minutes or until thickened, stirring constantly. Remove from the heat and stir in the vanilla and almond extract.

Sprinkle the sugar over the peaches in a bowl and let stand until the sugar dissolves. Arrange the pound cake slices to cover the bottom of a trifle dish. Brush generously with the liqueur. Layer one-third of the peaches and one-third of the custard over the cake. Repeat the layers until all the cake, peaches and custard are used.

Chill the trifle, covered, for 4 to 24 hours. Spread the whipped cream over the top and sprinkle with the almonds.

SERVES 10

Berrytini Mousse

1   (16-ounce) package frozen sweetened sliced
      strawberries, partially thawed
1   cup sour cream or light sour cream
$^1/_3$ cup sugar
1   tablespoon vanilla extract
1   cup whipped cream
      Red colored sugar
      Fresh strawberries or other berries, for garnish

Combine the strawberries, sour cream, sugar and vanilla in a blender and process until smooth. Fold in the whipped cream. Coat the rims of six to eight martini glasses with colored sugar. Spoon the berry mixture into the glasses. Freeze for 2 hours or longer.

Let stand at room temperature until slightly softened. Garnish with strawberries or other berries on martini picks.

Vary this recipe by substituting raspberries, blueberries or blackberries for the strawberries. The colored sugar can be found in the baking aisle of the grocery store. You can also color sugar with a drop or two of food coloring.

SERVES 6 TO 8

Blood Orange Tangerine Gelato

Scott McGehee, *Chef/Proprietor of Boulevard Bread Company*

7   cups fresh blood orange juice and/or tangerine juice
1¹/2 cups sugar

*C*ombine the juice with the sugar in an ice cream maker and mix to dissolve the sugar. Freeze using the manufacturer's directions. Sometimes the most delicious things can be so simple!

MAKES ABOUT 2 QUARTS

Coming Home to Arkansas

"My favorite thing about coming back to Arkansas is the way most people have embraced me so warmly. Through my music, acting, and teaching, I feel that God has brought me full circle. I am so pleased when I see a student 'get it' when I teach…or many enjoy a song that I sing…or just the wonderful people of this city and state who come over and just say hello. During my recent bout with cancer, the outpouring of love was amazing. I had wanted to just be private about the whole ordeal but when people found out, they showed and continue to show incredible love and support."

—Lawrence Hamilton
Broadway star and Arkansas native

Coconut Ice Cream

1	(12-ounce) can evaporated milk	1	(14-ounce) can coconut milk
1	(3-ounce) package coconut cream pudding and pie filling mix	2	cups half-and-half Toasted coconut and crushed
1	(14-ounce) can sweetened condensed milk		macadamia nuts, for garnish

Bring the evaporated milk to a simmer in a saucepan over medium heat. Whisk in the pudding mix and remove from the heat. Cool to room temperature.

Combine the condensed milk, coconut milk and half-and-half in a large bowl and mix well. Stir in the pudding mixture. Chill in the refrigerator for 30 minutes.

Pour into an ice cream maker and freeze using the manufacturer's directions. Spoon into dishes and garnish with toasted coconut and macadamia nuts.

MAKES ABOUT 2 QUARTS

Ice Cream Variations

The Coconut Ice Cream recipe above can be easily changed to your favorite flavor. For Chocolate Ice Cream, omit the coconut milk and substitute chocolate pudding mix for the coconut cream pudding mix. Melt one pound of semisweet chocolate into three cups of half-and-half and add to the pudding mixture. Freeze using the manufacturer's directions.

For Strawberry Ice Cream, combine four cups of ripe Arkansas strawberries with one cup of sugar and purée. Omit the coconut milk and substitute vanilla pudding mix for the coconut cream pudding mix, using three cups of half-and-half. Add the strawberries and freeze using the manufacturer's directions.

Seckel Pear Crème Brûlée

Lee Richardson, *Executive Chef of Capital Hotel*

3   Seckel pears
1/2   bottle sauterne or other sweet wine
3   cups heavy cream
1   cup milk
1/4   cup sugar
1   vanilla bean, split and scraped, or
       1 teaspoon vanilla extract
7   egg yolks
1/4   cup sugar

Cut the pears into halves lengthwise, taking care to cut straight through the center. Cut a thin slice from the rounded side so the pear halves will sit flat. Scoop out the interior of the pears, preserving the shape of the pears and the peel. Reserve the scooped-out portion for another use.

Combine the pear shells with the wine in a small saucepan. Cook over medium heat just until the pear shells begin to be translucent. Cool and drain. Arrange on a baking sheet.

Combine the cream, milk, 1/4 cup sugar and the vanilla bean in a saucepan. Cook over medium heat until bubbles appear around the edge of the saucepan. Whisk the egg yolks with 1/4 cup sugar in a bowl. Add the cream mixture to the egg yolks in a steady stream, whisking constantly.

Strain immediately into a cool container. Spoon carefully into the pear shells. Bake at 275 degrees for 20 minutes.

SERVES 6

Sticky Fingerz Banana Pudding

Suzon Awbrey, *Owner/Operator of Sticky Fingerz Rock-n-Roll Chicken Shack and Rumba Room*

1	large package banana instant pudding mix	2	tablespoons Frangelico
1	tablespoon butter	1	teaspoon cinnamon
3	bananas, sliced		Caramel sauce, warmed
1/2	cup packed brown sugar		Whipped cream, toasted pecans and vanilla wafer crumbs

Prepare the pudding mix using the package directions. Melt the butter in a sauté pan over medium heat. Add the bananas, brown sugar, liqueur and cinnamon. Sauté until the brown sugar dissolves and the bananas are coated. Add to the pudding and mix gently. Cool for 1 hour or longer. Coat individual serving cups with warm caramel sauce. Spoon the pudding into the cups. Top with whipped cream, toasted pecans and vanilla wafer crumbs. Drizzle additional warm caramel sauce over the top.

SERVES 6

White Chocolate Bread Pudding

4	cups heavy whipping cream	1	cup sugar
16	ounces French bread, torn into 1-inch pieces	2	tablespoons vanilla extract
3	eggs, lightly beaten	2	cups (12 ounces) white chocolate chips

Pour the cream over the bread in a bowl and let stand for 10 minutes. Combine the eggs, sugar and vanilla in a bowl and mix until smooth. Add to the bread and mix well into the bread; the mixture should not be soupy. Add a small amount of milk if the mixture is not moist enough. Stir in the white chocolate chips. Spoon into a 9×13-inch baking pan. Bake at 350 degrees for 45 minutes or until golden brown.

SERVES 8 TO 10

Performing Arts

The performing arts are lively and diverse in Central Arkansas. Savor the Arkansas Symphony as it annually schedules more than thirty concerts at the Robinson Center Music Hall. Laugh and cry at the Arkansas Repertory Theatre as it produces stunning performances in its own complex on Main Street. Ballet Arkansas and Arkansas Festival Ballet are candy for the eyes, while the River City Men's Chorus is a treat for the ears. Explore Wildwood Park for the Performing Arts in western Little Rock—one of the largest land areas devoted to the performances of opera, jazz, Broadway music, and more. Plus, watch for special entertaining events scheduled year-round at Robinson Center and at the University of Arkansas at Little Rock. Wherever you look, the curtain's going up!

Food and Wine Pairing Guidelines

- Acid neutralizes acid. For example, many salad dressings are vinaigrettes. If paired with a rich, buttery chardonnay, they taste off. If paired with a crisp sauvignon blanc with comparable acid to the vinaigrette, each complements the other.
- Light whites/reds with lighter cheeses.
- Fuller whites/reds with fuller cheeses.
- Salt neutralizes tannin. For example, take a sip of a great big California cabernet. Notice how the wine dominates your mouth. Take a few bites of some very salty tortilla chips, and then taste the cabernet again. The flavor disappears.
- Tannin and alcohol increase the spice in a dish. If the dish is very spicy, think about using a wine with lower alcohol and tannin. For example, German rieslings are great with Thai or Latin food, while cabernet is not.
- Dessert wines must be sweeter than the dessert.
- Match regional food with regional wines. Find out where a food originates—the best wines with that are most likely wines from the same region.

Some of the All-Time Best Food and Wine Matches

- Tomato sauce with chianti
- Steak fries with bordeaux
- Oysters with either Champagne or muscadet
- Stilton cheese with port
- Foie gras with sauternes
- Goat cheese with sauvignon blanc (especially Loire Valley, France)
- Pork and apples with German riesling

Some Other Helpful Tips

- Match color with color. Pork works better with white wine, and lamb and beef work better with reds.
- Weight considerations. If a dish is served with a rich white sauce, make sure the wine is a rich white wine. If beef is served without a sauce, use a light red. If a beef dish has a very flavorful sauce, serve with a more full-bodied red.

Measurement Equivalents

Teaspoons

3 teaspoons . . . . .1 tablespoon

Tablespoons

2 tablespoons . . . .^{1}/8 cup

4 tablespoons . . . .^{1}/4 cup

5 tablespoons plus 1 teaspoon . . . .^{1}/3 cup

8 tablespoons . . . .^{1}/2 cup

12 tablespoons . . . .^{3}/4 cup

16 tablespoons . . . . .1 cup

32 tablespoons . . . . .2 cups

64 tablespoons . . . . .1 quart

96 tablespoons . . . . .1^1/2 quarts

Ounces

1 ounce . . . . .2 tablespoons fat or liquid

4 ounces . . . .^{1}/2 cup

8 ounces . . . . .1 cup

16 ounces . . . . .1 pound

Cups, Pints, and Quarts

^{5}/8 cup . . . .^{1}/2 cup plus 2 tablespoons equals 10 tablespoons

^{7}/8 cup . . . .^{3}/4 cup plus 2 tablespoons equals 14 tablespoons

2 cups . . . . .1 pint

2 pints . . . . .1 quart

1 quart . . . . .4 cups

4 quarts . . . . .1 gallon

Ingredient Equivalents

Fruits

1 pound apples	=	3 medium or 3 cups sliced
1 cup chopped pitted dates or candied fruit	=	8 ounces
1 medium lemon	=	3 tablespoons juice
1 medium lemon	=	1 tablespoon grated zest
1 medium lime	=	2 tablespoons juice
1 medium lime	=	1 teaspoon grated zest
1 orange	=	$^1/_3$ cup juice
1 orange	=	2 tablespoons grated zest
4 cups sliced peaches	=	8 medium
$1^3/_4$ cups sliced berries	=	1 pint

Meats

3 cups chopped cooked meat	=	1 pound cooked
2 cups ground cooked meat	=	1 pound cooked

Milk and Cream

1 cup whipping cream	=	2 cups whipped cream
1 (8-ounce) carton sour cream	=	1 cup sour cream

Vegetables

1 (4-ounce) can mushrooms	=	$^1/_2$ pound fresh
1 pound fresh mushrooms	=	6 cups sliced
1 chopped medium onion	=	$^1/_2$ cup
1 chopped large onion	=	1 cup
1 cup shelled fresh peas	=	1 pound
3 medium potatoes	=	1 pound or 3 cups chopped
$2^1/_2$ cups cooked fresh tomatoes	=	4 medium or 1 pound
1 tablespoon fresh herbs	=	1 teaspoon dried

Glossary of Cooking Terms

If you are an experienced cook, you won't need this, but if you're less experienced, it will give you a good starting place.

B

Bake—To cook by dry heat in an oven or under hot coals.

Baste—To moisten, especially meats, with melted butter, pan drippings, sauce, etc., during cooking time.

Beat—To mix ingredients by vigorous stirring or with an electric mixer.

Blanch—To immerse, usually vegetables or fruit, briefly into boiling water to inactivate enzymes, loosen skin, or soak away excess salt.

Blend—To combine 2 or more ingredients, at least 1 of which is liquid or soft, to quickly produce a mixture of uniform consistency.

Boil—To heat liquid until bubbly; the boiling point for water is about 212 degrees, depending on altitude and atmospheric pressure.

Braise—To cook, especially meats, covered, in a small amount of liquid.

Brew—To prepare a beverage by allowing boiling water to extract flavor and/or color from certain substances.

Broil—To cook by direct exposure to intense heat, such as a flame or an electric heating unit.

C

Caramelize—To melt sugar in a heavy pan over low heat until golden brown, stirring constantly.

Chill—To cool in the refrigerator or in cracked ice.

Clarify—To remove impurities from melted butter by allowing the sediment to settle, then pouring off clear yellow liquid. Other fats may be clarified by straining.

Cream—To blend butter, margarine, shortening, or sometimes oil with a granulated or crushed ingredient until the mixture is soft and creamy. Usually described in method as light and fluffy. Butter and margarine are usually softened first.

Curdle—To congeal milk with rennet or heat until solid lumps or curds are formed.

Cut in—To disperse solid shortening into dry ingredients with a knife or pastry blender. The texture of the mixture should resemble coarse cracker meal. Described in method as crumbly.

D

Deep-fry—To cook in a deep pan or skillet containing hot cooking oil. Deep-fried foods are generally completely immersed in the hot oil.

Deglaze—To heat stock, wine, or other liquid in the pan in which meat has been cooked, mixing with pan drippings and sediment to form a gravy or sauce base.

Dice—To cut into small cubes about one-quarter-inch size.

Dissolve—To create a solution by thoroughly mixing a solid or granular substance with a liquid.

Dredge—To coat completely with flour, bread crumbs, etc.

F

Fillet—To remove bones from meat or fish; or a boneless piece of fish, meat, or chicken.

Flambé—To pour warmed brandy or other spirits over food in a pan, and then ignite and continue cooking briefly.

Fold in—To blend a delicate frothy mixture into a heavier one so that none of the lightness of volume is lost. Using a rubber spatula, turn under and bring up and over, rotating bowl 1/4 turn after each motion.

Fry—To cook in a pan or skillet containing hot cooking oil. The oil should not totally cover the food.

G

Garnish—To decorate food before serving.

Glaze—To cover or coat with sauce, syrup, egg white, or a jellied substance. After applying, it becomes firm—adding color and flavor.

Grate—To rub food against a rough, perforated utensil to produce slivers, chunks, curls, etc.

Grill—To broil, usually over hot coals or charcoal.

Grind—To cut, crush, or force through a chopper to produce small bits.

I–L

Infuse—To steep herbs or other flavorings in a liquid until the liquid absorbs flavor.

Julienne—To cut vegetables, fruit, etc., into long thin strips.

Knead—To press, fold, and stretch dough until smooth and elastic. Method usually notes time frame or result.

Leaven—To cause batters and doughs to rise, usually by means of a chemical leavening agent. This process may occur before or during baking.

M

Marinate—To soak, usually in a highly seasoned oil-acid solution, to flavor and/or tenderize food.

Melt—To liquefy solid foods by the action of heat.

Mince—To cut or chop into very small pieces.

M

Mix—To combine ingredients to distribute uniformly.

Mold—To shape into a particular form.

P

Panfry—To cook in a skillet or pan containing only a small amount of fat.

Parboil—To partially cook in boiling water. Most parboiled foods require additional cooking.

Pit—To remove the hard inedible seed from peaches, plums, etc.

Plank—To broil and serve on a board or wooden platter.

Plump—To soak fruits, usually dried, in liquid until puffy and softened.

Poach—To cook in a small amount of gently simmering liquid.

Preserve—To prevent food spoilage by pickling, salting, dehydrating, smoking, boiling in syrup, etc. Preserved foods have excellent keeping qualities. Be sure method of canning uses USDA approved standards.

Purée—To reduce the pulp of cooked fruit and vegetables to a smooth and thick liquid by straining or blending.

R

Reduce—To boil stock, gravy, or other liquid until volume is reduced, liquid is thickened, and flavor is intensified.

Refresh—To place blanched drained vegetables or other food in cold water to halt the cooking process.

Render—To cook meat or meat trimmings at low temperature until fat melts and can be drained and strained.

Roast—(1) To cook by dry heat either in an oven or over hot coals. (2) To dry or parch by intense heat.

S

Sauté—To cook in a skillet containing a small amount of hot cooking oil. Sautéed foods should never be immersed in the oil. Should be stirred frequently.

Scallop—To bake with a sauce in a casserole. The food may either be mixed or layered with the sauce.

Score—To make shallow cuts diagonally in parallel lines, especially meat.

Scramble—To cook and stir simultaneously, especially eggs.

Shred—To cut or shave food into slivers.

Shuck—To remove the husk from corn or the shell from oysters, clams, etc.

Sieve—To press a mixture through a coarsely meshed metal utensil to make it homogeneous.

Sift—To pass, usually dry ingredients, through a fine wire mesh to produce a uniform consistency.

Simmer—To cook in or with a liquid at or just below the boiling point.

Skewer—(1) To thread—usually meat and vegetables—onto a sharpened rod (as in shish kabob). (2) To fasten the opening of stuffed fowl closed with small pins.

Skim—To ladle or spoon off excess fat or scum from the surface of a liquid.

Smoke—To preserve or cook through continuous exposure to wood smoke for a long time.

Steam—To cook with water vapor in a closed container, usually in a steamer, on a rack, or in a double boiler.

Sterilize—To cleanse and purify through exposure to intense heat.

Stew—To simmer—usually meats and vegetables—for a long period of time. Also used to tenderize meats.

Stir-fry—To cook small pieces of vegetables and/or meat in a small amount of oil in a wok or skillet over high heat until tender-crisp, stirring constantly. Popular Asian technique.

Strain—To pass through a strainer, sieve, or cheesecloth to break down or remove solids or impurities.

Stuff—To fill or pack cavities, especially those of meats, vegetables, and poultry.

T

Toast—To brown and crisp, usually by means of direct heat, or to bake until brown.

Truss—To bind poultry legs and wings close to body before cooking.

W

Whip—To beat a mixture until air has been thoroughly incorporated and the mixture is light and fluffy, volume is greatly increased, and the mixture holds its shape.

Wilt—To apply heat to cause dehydration and a droopy appearance.

Contributors

Amy Abdella
Gen Abdella
Kem Aburrow
Kristin Aburrow
Dawn Adams
Judy Adams
Rickie Adams
Kimberly Aitkens
Margaret Albright
Marsha McNeil Allbritton
Becky Allred
Jan Alman
Susan Altrui
Ann Anderson
Charlotte Satterfield Anderson
Missy Anderson
Christine Buettner Appleton
Marystel Appleton
Jennie Marie Ashford
Jean Ashmore
Rayni Ashmore
Sharon Aureli
Suzon Awbrey
Elizabeth Aymond
Debi Bagley
Linda Balch
Amy Ballard
Karen Ballheimer
Tricia Ballheimer
Nancy Banks
Amber Barham
Jennifer Barrett
Linda Barry
Lisa Baxter
Trudy Baxter
Anna Benson
Rita Benson
Byron Birch
Linda Butler Bishop
Ginger Blackmon
Sydney Blackmon
Katherine Blackmon-Solis
Pam Blank
Buff Blass

Georgia Bobo
Kelleigh Ann Boerner
Meme Bogan
Terri Bonner
Celia Boon
Faye Borgman
Christy Bourns
Mary Lynn Bourns
Aza Bowlin
Kimberly Bowman
Melissa Bradley
Erin Brady
Juli Brandenberger
Peter Brave
Leigh Ashley Breedlove
Brook Brewer
Pam Bridges
Tiffany Bright
Chris Brown
Wendie Jill Brown
Betty Bumpers
Senator Dale Bumpers
Lovenia Burch
Elizabeth Burns
Joanna Butler
Katherine Butler
Sharon Butler
Emily West Bynum
Stephanie Bynum
Cathy Calloway
Margaret Calloway
Becky Campbell
Natalie Capps
Wanda Carley
Jean Carlisle
Kathy Carlisle
Scott Whiteley Carter
Connie Carty
Amy West Chandler
Michelle Cheek
Courtney Childers
Laura Christensen
Shelley Chumley
Elizabeth Clark

President Bill Clinton
Bo Clinton
Senator Hillary Clinton
Susie Cook
Lindsay Coon
Ann Cooper
Jennie Coy
Karen Coy
Kate Crain
Leigh Ann Crain
Tara D. Crain
Frances Cranford
Jay Cranford
Ross Cranford
Charlene Creech
Barbara Crews
Julia Crow
Jackie Crowder
Elizabeth Crowson
Pam Crowson
Kerri Daniels
Natalie Darnell
Michelle Davenport
Cindy Davis
Connie Davis
Tammie Davis
Erin Dees
Linda Deloney
Phyllis Dickerson
Laura Dickinson
Sharon Die
Lyndsey Dilks
Marian Dinkins-Armstrong
Peyton Lee Dobrovich
Laura Doramus
Karen Dottley
Cathy Dougherty
Robert Dougherty
Shermaine Dowling
Heather Drew
Missy Duke
Lurlie Jones Dykes
Mary Carolyn East
Thomas Collier East

Aminah Eddings
Lee Edwards
Leah Elenzweig
Neil Elenzweig
Carrie Brady Faletti
Katherine Faulk
Rosella D. Faulk
Jenny Faulkner
Lizzy Faulkner
Margaret Faulkner
Josephine Hoover Felton
Annie Feltus
Cindy Feltus
Robert Feltus
Donnie Ferneau
J.T. Ferstl
Jamie Fields
Anita Fiser
Debby Fiser
Jennifer Forrest
Valerie Fortner
Elizabeth Fortune
Brigita Gardner
Nancy Gardner
Molly Gathright
Debi Gefell
Amber Gibbons
Melissa Godfrey
Nicole Good
Barbara Graves
Julie Greathouse
Ernest G. Green
Tisha Gribble
Stacy Grobmyer
Amanda Groce
Beverly Guerrero
Kristina Gulley
Ashley Gunderman
Dori Haddock
Audrey Hairston
James Hale
Ann Hall
Dr. Lillian Hall
Helen B. Hall

Whitnie Hall
Jeane Hamilton
Lawrence Hamilton
Ryan Hamra
Susan Harbour
Jana Harris
Ashley Harry
Jill Hartsfield
Kimberly Hartsfield
Heather Haywood
Emily Heard
Cheryl Helms
Donna Helms
Margaret Helms
Mirl Helms
Ruby Henderson
Johnnie Henry
Kathryn Hall Henry
Martha Blackwell Hestand
Allison Hester
Anne Hickman
Holley Hickman
Sara M. Hickman
Sara Schrekenhofer Hickman
Ellen Hill
Kyle Orr Hinson
Dana Hof
Tiffany Hoffman
Mrs. E.G. Hoover
Scott Hotzhouser
Yolanda Hugg
Shannon Hughen
Lee Humble
Mimi Hurst
Stacey Hurst
Annesley Hussey
Edwin Hussey
Julia Hussey
Kathleen Hussey
Judy Irwin
Adele Cashion Jackson
Becca Jackson
Beverly Jackson
John Richard Jackson

Meggan Jackson
Susan Jackson
Mary Sue Jacobs
Kelley Jansen
Anne Jarrard
Angie Johnson
Emily Hunter Johnson
Jordan Johnson
Lucy Johnson
Stephanie Johnson
Andrea Johnston
Jessica Johnston-Myers
Jamie Huffman Jones
Janet Jones
Emily Jordan-Cox
Abigail West Jumper
Karen Junot
Joyce Kaemmerling
Marcia Kahn
Sarah Kahn
Sherri Kelley
Gloria Kemp
Grace Kennon
Melanie Kennon
Denyse Killgore
Katie Kirkpatrick
JoJo Kittell
Louise Kline
Jason Knapp
Rachel Cook Knox
Ellen Kornblat
Leslie Korte
Lauren Kreps
Naomi Kryske
Amy Kurczek
Gail Lackey
Kristen Lamb
Jenny Landes
Martha Landes
Cherry Landfair
Lindsey Laney
Kristin Larsson
Amy Lasley
Roxie Lawrence

Jeanne Ledbetter
Charlotte Volk Lee
Helen Lee
Mara Leveritt
Senator Blanche Lincoln
Dale Linton
Debby Linton
Dennis Little
Sally Green Little
Trena Lunsford
Marge Anna Luttrell
Mara Malcolm
Diana Markatos
Mary Margaret Rasco Marks
Natasha Marlow
Susan Marshall
Carmen Martina
Kathryn Martinez
Samaria Mascagni
Ron Maxwell
Beth McAlpine
Catherine McBride
Nicole McCain
Carolyn McCarley
JoBeth McElhanon
Scott McGehee
Shannon McKinney
Betty McLain
Megan McLean
Emily McMath
Mary McMillan
Tiffani Mendivil
Christine Menking
Vickey Metrailer
Cindy Miller
Kristen Minton
Tracy Mitchell
Lynn Monk
Susannah Monk
Enrrietthy Monterrey
Blanche Moore
Jewel Moore
Mary Morgan
Timothy Morton

William D. Moss
Natasha Naragon
Ora Neeley
Dixie Rodgers Noonan
Paul Novicky
April Null
Ashley O'Brien
Inez O'Brien
Paula O'Brien
Susan Odom
Ashley Olinghouse
Anne Wynne O'Neill
Brooke Augusta Owen
Marilyn Owen
Mary Owen
Anne Pace
Deidra Parish
Ashley Parker
Camille Parker
Kay Payne
Amy Peck
Jill Penick
Kathy Perkins
Jason Pettie
Fred Phillips
Melanie Phillips
Mandy Keaton Piechocki
Andre Poirot
Velma Prall
Meredith Price
Sarah Priebe
Erin Propst
Jeanie Pruss
Senator Mark Pryor
Katherine Raborn
Jan Ragland
Carol H. Rasco
Trenda Ray
Leann Reed
Melody Rhodes
Mary Adcox Rice
Amanda Richardson
Lee Richardson
Mary Melekian Richardson

Scott Rittlelmeyer
Lesley Landes Roberts
Jennifer Robinson
Ron Robinson
Tiffany Robinson
Jane Rogers
Jill Rogers
Ayelette Roper
Dorothy Ross
Jo Ross
Nancy Rousseau
Billie Rutherford
Skip Rutherford
Leslie Rutledge
Nancy Rutledge
Crissy San Roman
Lee San Roman
Lindsey Prather Sanders
Kerri Sangalli
Barbara Satterfield
Julianne Satterfield
Beth Scanlan
Vicki Scanlon
Lin Schuster
Brenda Scissons
Susan Scott
Susannah Scruggs
Nita Secuban
Jennifer Selig
John Selig
Judy Selig
Michael Selig
Antoine Seyer
Paula Sharp
Matsy Shea
Jancey Sheats
Katherine Shell
Lori Shemper
Jimmie Shepherd
Sandra Shepherd
Betsy Shollmier
Genie Sigler
Amy Simpkins
Elaine Small

Sarah Smart
Clayton Smith
Jo Atkins Smith
Kathy Smith
Michelle R. Smith
Larua Snavely
Nan Snow
Representative Vic Snyder
Megan Sprigler
April Stephens
Sherrise Stephens
Anne Stermock
Mary Stermock
Marian Steward
Griffin Stockley
Stephanie Streett
Sarah Stringer
Anna Strong
Julie Tabor
Catherine Tapp
Imogene Taylor
Debbie Teague

Anne Tedford
Louise Terzia
Megan Thornton
Rett Tucker
Shelly Tucker
Melissa Tyler
Jennie Van Es
Annella Van Zandt
Mike Vangness
Kathleen Velek
Catherine Vest
Lynette Vinson
Laura Beth Vogel
LuAnne Vogel
Audrey Urfer Volk
Aaron Wage
Barbara Wagner
Danyelle J. Walker
Babs Wardlaw
Tiffany Warriner
Irene Wassall
Haven Waters

Marcia Watkins
Traci Weaver
Kathy Webb
Karen Welch
Mary Lee Welch
Katherine West
Alleta Wiggins
Brooke Wilkerson
Terrie Wilkerson
Kathy Wilkins
Jackie Williams
Marty Koehler Williams
Maxine Williams
Regina Williams
Izora Wilson
Priscilla Pen Wilson
Rosemary Wilson
Angela Winston
Barbara Woods
Dana Yates
Emily Young
Maggie Young

Junior League of Little Rock Board of Directors

2007–2008

Tammie Davis, *President*
JoBeth McElhanon, *President-Elect*
Jana Harris, *Administrative Vice-President*
Beth McAlpine, *Community Vice-President*
Debbie Teague, *Development Vice-President*
Dania Garner, *Marketing Vice-President*
Courtney McLarty, *Membership Vice-President*
Jennifer Pierce, *Treasurer*
Amy Kurczek, *Treasurer-Elect*
Julianne Satterfield, *Nominating Chair*
Karen Fetzer, *Sustainer Advisor*

2008–2009

JoBeth McElhanon, *President*
Courtney McLarty, *President-Elect*
Melanie Hoover, *Administrative Vice-President*
Ashley Olinghouse, *Community Vice-President*
Jennifer Pierce, *Development Vice-President*
Tisha Gribble, *Marketing Vice-President*
Missy Duke, *Membership Vice-President*
Amy Kurczek, *Treasurer*
Becka Webb, *Treasurer-Elect*
Ellen Hill, *Nominating Chair*
Mimi Hurst, *Sustainer Advisor*

Index

BIG TASTE OF LITTLE ROCK

Big Taste of Little Rock

For additional copies of

Big Taste of Little Rock

or for order information on *Little Rock Cooks, Traditions,* and *Apron Strings,*
please contact

Junior League of Little Rock
501.375.5557
www.jllr.org